A Memoir on the Ot ⸺gy Renaissance

JUST ANOTHER IMMIGRANT'S SON

Michael M. Paparella, MD

with Nicole Helget

BEAVER'S POND
PRESS

Edited by Wendy Weckwerth.

ISBN 13: 978-1-59298-615-6
Library of Congress Catalog Number: 2019906704
Printed in the United States of America
First Printing: 2020
24 23 22 21 20   5 4 3 2 1

Cover and interior design by Dan Pitts.

BEAVER'S POND PRESS

Beaver's Pond Press, Inc.
939 Seventh Street West,
Saint Paul, MN 55102
(952) 829-8818
www.BeaversPondPress.com

To order, visit www.ItascaBooks.com. Reseller discounts available.

To my family, students, patients, and mentors.
And my country.

Human Ear Diagram

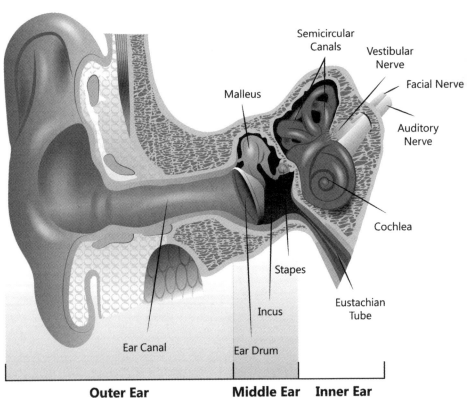

Semicircular Canals

Vestibular Nerve

Facial Nerve

Malleus

Auditory Nerve

Cochlea

Stapes

Incus

Eustachian Tube

Ear Canal

Ear Drum

Outer Ear   **Middle Ear**   **Inner Ear**

Contents

Foreword

It has been said that life is so complex it's difficult to tell the good news from the bad. Should we laugh or cry? Retreat or push forward?

Perhaps that's how an optimist regards himself—not a mere Pollyanna but rather someone who refuses to think in terms of gain or loss. The optimist shies away from labeling news as good or bad but instead views any news as another opportunity inviting change. When life gives you lemons, you make a lemon meringue pie, or maybe a lemon soufflé. And, if times are lean and the larder is bare, you can always do lemonade.

I first met Michael Paparella forty-seven years ago in his small, simple sixth-floor office in the Mayo Memorial Building at the University of Minnesota Medical School. On a blustery, wintry afternoon, he interviewed me as a young and sweaty-palmed residency applicant. We formed a bond right from the start. We were both from Detroit, when it was a nicer and gentler city. We both attended the University of Michigan as undergraduates and for medical school. We both loved ENT (ear, nose, and throat) practice, and we both realized that ENT was embarking on a scientific renaissance in front of our very eyes. It was obvious to me then that he was, and remains, a card-carrying and inveterate optimist.

On top of that, Michael Paparella is a curious explorer. Sir Edmund Hillary scaled forbidding peaks. Leonardo da Vinci dreamed of machines that never were. In

1967 Michael Paparella was the youngest ENT department chair in the country; he was just starting out, but he was determined to be in fraternity with these forerunners. As I watched Michael Paparella mature throughout his career, I noticed that he was always asking questions. He sought out surprises, and even when a surprise might have frightened him or others, he allowed himself to respond with unconventional thinking and purposely set aside time to exercise his curiosity. This latter endeavor is often called "going to the lab."

Michael Paparella dared to differ when he thought it would benefit his patients or medical science. He appreciates novelty, and he broke away from the pack in medical school because he knew the renaissance in ENT was at hand. Any renaissance is disquieting and uncomfortable because of its inherent unknowns, and staying with the status quo of surgical science would have been less risky for him. But it made no sense to look back and imitate the past when he could peer into the enticing future. He formulated new medical ideas by troubleshooting, by trial and error, and by working to solve the failures of old or antiquated treatments and surgical procedures.

When I was a brand-new ENT resident, Michael Paparella hustled me off to the otopathology lab one afternoon and taught me how to read temporal bone sections with a binocular microscope. He was convinced that patients who had aggressive forms of leukemia were experiencing disastrous complications deep inside their ears. I spent many days in the lab checking out his notion— and then getting home much later on those lab nights because there was no reprieve from all the undone patient-admission workups still waiting on the wards. He was right about the leukemia problem. I compiled the research data into a paper, and he let me present it at a national meeting. Imagine that! A renowned chair let me steal his thunder. The presentation in Saint Louis went well, and even though I was an ENT neophyte, I received congratulatory letters (only snail mail then) from notable chairs around the country. The study was Michael Paparella's idea, but he welcomed, even rejoiced in, my interest in his project. It was called teaching. Perhaps that's his biggest and best legacy. He wanted to pass on what he was discovering. And, he wanted to convince others to be always intellectually curious—to discover and pass it all on too. That explains his extraordinary accomplishment in fostering the next generation of new and curious thinkers in ENT—many of whom, predictably, became professors and chairs around the world. Yes, the world. And now they're fostering another generation.

The way he approaches his personal life is the way he approaches his professional life. He's admired and befriended for his noncritical attitudes, his applause for curiosity, his tolerance of anxiety and uncertainty, his sense of humor and playfulness, and his typically warm Italian emotions.

The privilege of a lifetime is being who you are. Michael Paparella was granted that privilege, and he worked hard to make sure he grabbed its full measure. Now please turn the page and meet this remarkable man.

—Dr. Norman Berlinger, MD, PhD, Minneapolis, 2019

The Otology Renaissance

I, the son of Italian immigrants, am a very lucky guy. Born in America, the great land of opportunity, I had good parents, a supportive community, many formidable bosses, a rigorous education, and a lineage of wise mentors. Ultimately, all these factors contributed to my career as an otolaryngologist, which is a big word for an ear, nose, and throat doctor, with a specialty in otology and neurotology, which are fancy words for "the study of the anatomy and diseases of the ear and their related neurological disorders."

The inner ear, which is smaller than your small fingernail, consists of the spiraled cochlea in front (which relays the noises we hear to the brain) and the vestibular labyrinth in the back. When diseased, the vestibular labyrinth can cause serious problems, such as incapacitating vertigo in Ménière's disease, among many others. The inner ear is protected by one of the hardest bones in the human body, the temporal bone. It acts like a safe as it protects those very delicate intricacies of the ear, including the sensory cells for hearing, the sensory cells for balance, and the attached stapes, which is the smallest bone in the human body.

Ear problems are so common it sometimes feels that we accept them as an unavoidable part of the life cycle. Little Maria's ear hurts again. Get her an antibiotic. Uncle Joe is deaf as a doorknob. Yell in his face when you talk to him.

What I've learned over my decades of study, though, is that each of these people is unique and has to be properly diagnosed. And, what's affecting their comfort and ability to hear has to be understood before it can be properly treated. I've been so fortunate to be a witness to and a participant in what could be called the renaissance of otology, a relatively brief period of time, maybe two to three decades, during which key discoveries were made in ear and hearing research, top otologists were educated and advanced teaching in the field, and vital clinical and surgical contributions were developed to significantly improve the lives of thousands, indeed millions, of patients with a variety of ear diseases. Little Maria doesn't have to have chronic ear infections. Uncle Joe can hear again.

Ear diseases have all sorts of causes, including congenital, genetic, cancerous, and traumatic. Some symptoms of ear disease are so serious that patients think they're going crazy or honestly wish to die rather than live another day with the disorientation and incapacitating dizziness. Approximately forty million Americans have a significant hearing loss or deafness and/or tinnitus, an onomatopoeic term that means *unwanted ear ringing*. A shocking ninety million Americans suffer from dizziness or vertigo, according to studies conducted by the National Institutes of Health (NIH). If you've ever imbibed too much wine and then attempted to lie down, only to feel as though the room was spinning wildly and sucking you down into a whirlpool, you'll understand what it's like for people who live with this symptom. It's sickening. It's nauseating. It's unsettling. Vertigo is usually due to an inner-ear disease.

And who among us doesn't recall the childhood misery of ear infections? They are so common, a whole book of home remedies could be compiled. I've heard of parents who used olive oil drops and those who used cotton balls soaked in Vicks VapoRub. I've heard of dads blowing cigarette smoke into the ear canal of the suffering child and moms who warm salt in a tube sock and press it against the child's ear. Parents will try almost anything to relieve a child in pain. Almost all children will have otitis media, an ear infection, prior to age five, and approximately 10 percent of children will have chronic ear infections with fluid behind the eardrum and hearing loss, which is curable if the problem is treated promptly.

New knowledge and technology have helped my colleagues and me treat our patients who have devastating ear diseases. In most instances, they've had hearing restored, vertigo eliminated, and other diseases cured or improved. Our patients who need surgery usually go home the same day, and the results are generally very good. In fact, for most patients, the results are amazing because they go on to fully enjoy their lives. I've been told many times: "Doc, you gave me my life back."

I have been a doctor in otolaryngology and otology from 1961 to the present, which happens to parallel the renaissance of otology. This period, plus slightly earlier, yielded the most medical, surgical, and technological developments in the history of ear diseases dating back to primitive man.

Many giants of the medical field made important earlier contributions to the developing understanding and treatment of ear diseases. We can look back even further, back into the antiquity, back to the Mayan civilization in South America, which made ear drawings on a clinic hut ruin. The Egyptians three thousand years ago and the Persians and Chinese as many as six thousand years ago were making crude attempts to treat ear disease. Sometimes a doctor poked a stick in the ear to help relieve pain or infection or they purged blood and prescribed mercury or tried to syringe excess wax out of the ear. When it comes to the treatments of ear ailments, we're lucky to be alive in this day and age rather than theirs. But even in their rough ways, these activities all contributed to the understanding of how the ear works, its anatomy, and the problems associated with it. Trial and error in treatments, however unenlightened, slowly advanced the field.

At the turn of the twentieth century, otopathology was emphasized by the leading professors in Europe with painstaking drawings describing the histology (the study of the cells and tissues) and histopathology (the study of the nature of diseases), including sensory cells in cases of temporal bone diseases.

In the late nineteenth century, Dr. Adam Politzer made many contributions to the field as a professor at the University of Vienna in Austria. Ear doctors from the United States and other countries would visit Austria to study with him. His publications and contributions were numerous. Another important contribution developed for the surgical treatment of otosclerosis, which is a fixation of the stapes by bone, in the late 1930s and early 1940s. A colorful figure named Julius Lempert, sometimes called the Father of Otology, developed the first one-stage operation for deafness due to otosclerosis; it was called the fenestration operation (the development of a window into the inner ear via a mastoid operation). Lempert was born in Poland. At the ripe age of thirteen, he was arrested for protesting. His parents moved him and his sisters to Manhattan. Years later, Lempert became a doctor, and he practiced an assembly-line style of operating. This made him quite rich. Still, he continued to research and practice, ultimately focusing on the ear. He became a guru of sorts, inviting select otologists and researchers to visit him and learn. He also entertained them at New York City's famous 21 Club, where expensive cigars and dinners were enjoyed. Lempert supported research years before the NIH did.

Another major development in treating otitis media and chronic otitis media, which is a more serious chronic infection with tumor-like tissue, occurred with the discovery of penicillin, originally made from mold by Alexander Fleming. Penicillin was first used for ear infections in 1941. Before antibiotics, when children or adults had acute mastoiditis (an infection of the mastoid bone behind the ear), the major treatment was to drain the mastoid surgically. Ouch.

It might be said that the heart of the renaissance of otology started in the mid-1950s, with the most important innovations occurring from around 1955 to around 1985. The beginning of this renaissance coincides with a surgical microscope developed by the Zeiss Company in Germany. It was introduced and used for tympanoplasty, mastoid surgery, and all types of surgeries by German physicians Horst L. Wullstein in Würzburg and Fritz Zöllner in Freiberg. Eventually, surgical microscopes were used in other fields of surgery. Using microscopic methods meant for the first time a surgery, for cholesteatoma of the ear, for example, wasn't only designed for removal of pathology—but also, through microscopic methods, to reconstruct the middle ear with a grafted eardrum to retain or improve hearing. You can imagine many modifications by an array of ear experts followed Wullstein's and Zöllner's pioneering work.

Another development in the mid-1950s was the reintroduction of stapes surgery for deafness due to otosclerosis, which had been attempted unsuccessfully during the nineteenth century. While performing a fenestration operation under local anesthesia, Dr. Sam Rosen, an ear surgeon based in New York City, inadvertently bumped into the stapes. The patient said, "Stop, I can hear!" So Rosen stopped the operation and sent the patient on his way. He performed many stapes mobilization procedures thereafter. Unfortunately, hearing improvement was not sustained in most of these patients. Therefore, in 1956, Dr. John Shea of Memphis, Tennessee, reintroduced stapedectomy; aided by a microscope, he removed the stapes through the ear canal. Then he replaced the stapes with a prosthesis, so sounds could once again travel to the brain. Most of Shea's patients developed normal hearing or experienced significant improvement. Again, many refinements of treatments and techniques followed.

The story goes that Vincent van Gogh used a razor to cut off part of his ear during the Christmas season of 1888. Plagued by depression, mania, and "fits," he lopped it off, wrapped the ear in a cloth, and walked to a local bar. There, he presented the package to a prostitute, causing her to faint. Then he walked home and nearly bled to death in his bed before he was found unconscious and his wound was treated. Later, evoking that bloody incident, he painted himself with a large bandage around his head. At the age of thirty-seven the "mad genius" who was thought to be an epileptic and a lunatic, shot himself to death. Many modern scholars and doctors think Van Gogh actually suffered from Ménière's disease.

In 1927, Dr. Michel Portmann, a famous ear professor in Bordeaux, France, first performed an operation for patients with severe symptoms of Ménière's disease—deafness, vertigo, hearing loss, pressure, and tinnitus. Ménière's disease is a cursed ailment. For those who struggle with it, daily life can be hell on earth. As in Van Gogh's case, the disease was often misdiagnosed, mistreated, and so tormenting that some patients questioned whether they could live with it at all.

The most important, multiple major contributions to otology to treat that disease and others were made by Dr. William F. House of Los Angeles, California, a member of the world-renowned House Institute, founded by his otologist brother, Dr. Howard P. House. In the late 1950s and early 1960s, William House redeveloped and reintroduced a procedure called endolymphatic sac surgery. This is the only conservative operation for Ménière's disease, and it has benefited thousands of patients to date.

Significantly, William House also developed the field of skull base surgery—for example, using a surgical microscope to remove tumors, in the corner of the brain next to the ear. Many patients have had successful and more conservative surgery than was possible with previous intracranial approaches used by neurosurgeons. Other skull base diseases, such as glomus tumors, also could be treated with this important development. Another of House's most significant contributions to the field was the development of the first cochlear implant. His initial design has since undergone technological developments, and thousands who were deaf from various causes—too deaf for a hearing aid—have experienced hearing restoration with a cochlear implant.

One example is Rush Limbaugh, a successful radio host who became completely deaf from an autoimmune disease. Since his bilateral cochlear implantation, he has been able to continue his daily conservative talk show at a salary of fifty million dollars a year.

Most patients with hearing loss have a nerve-related type of hearing loss or sensorineural hearing loss, and a hearing aid is the only and best way to help them. The development of technology, including that of hearing aids, witnessed its zenith during the otology renaissance. They are much more sophisticated—and smaller and more functional than ever. Hearing aid development advanced simultaneously with the growth of Silicon Valley industries. Silicon chips have been integrated into hearing aids, to the benefit of deaf children and adults. Minneapolis is something of a center for hearing aid developments, because many hearing aid manufacturing companies originally started here. In fact, the largest hearing aid company in the United States, based in the Twin Cities, is Starkey Laboratories.

Audiometers are used to measure and diagnose hearing in various ways, and they have also improved considerably. Audiologists measure hearing losses, whether caused by problems from the external, middle, or inner ear. They also help measure vestibular function and dysfunction (using VNG, videonystagmography) and help diagnose cases of dizziness and vertigo. A previous method to test the vestibular system was to use buckets of hot and cold water, which were poured into the ear canal of patients. Can you imagine a child tolerating such a thing?

I had the idea, which I tested with a prototype, that hot and cold air could be used for more ear problems and with a lot less discomfort. Working with engineers in Chicago, I developed an air caloric machine, which can be tolerated by children and adults for a variety of vestibular and other ear diseases. These are now in common use worldwide.

An extremely important development occurred during the otology renaissance: financial support for otological research from the United States government. Before the renaissance there was little or no such funding. In the early years of the renaissance, limited support for deafness and communicative disorders was provided under the aegis of the Neurological Institute. I served on the NIH board at that time and while funds for deafness and communicative disorders research were limited, two of us representing otolaryngology—Dr. David Lim and myself—were able to provide additional financial support for grants, while receiving understanding and support from the other board members. Later, our own NIH Institute developed the National Institutes of Deafness and Communicative Disorders (NIDCD). While its budget exceeds four hundred million dollars, this amount is seriously insufficient and supports a small amount of the many excellent grants that have merit but cannot be funded. Including private foundations that support research, of which there are only a few, total support for otological research is grossly inadequate. I hope that federal financial support will more appropriately meet the needs of research in the future.

The renaissance also spawned a new generation of researchers and educators, and thereby leaps in research, publications, and educational techniques. Whether educating medical students, residents, or fellows, otology was taught with these remarkable developments in mind. Residency and fellowship training in otology increased during this period of time. Two types of fellows have been trained in the program at the Paparella Ear, Head and Neck Institute (in association with the International Hearing Foundation and the University of Minnesota), and other programs have a similar structure. Clinical fellows work along with physicians in an apprenticeship model in the Paparella Clinic. National and international research fellows come primarily to work in the Otopathology Laboratory at the University of Minnesota, but they can also observe clinical care activities. These are individuals who often go on to become leaders in the field after completing their fellowships, achieving professorships, becoming department chairs and even medical school deans.

While innovative clinical care, including operations for otosclerosis and chronic ear infection, have resulted from trial and error with a splash of serendipity, the basis of otology is research, whether it be basic or clinical (translational). Basic research seeks to understand the way the ear (temporal bone) functions in health and disease, and it involves almost every scientific discipline, including molecular biology, microbiology, stem cell research, and so on.

With good clinical corollary information, otohistopathological research represents the best and only way to see the pathology under the microscope. This research helps identify the cause and other related information that significantly assists in the diagnosis, understanding, and treatment of all ear diseases. For example, pathogenesis—which includes the cause of the disease, the mechanisms that lead to the pathology, and the clinical symptoms that lead the patient to see the otologist—is best studied by looking at sequential episodes of temporal bone slides to understand the disease and, better yet, how to treat it. Moreover, new diseases have been identified through otopathological research.

During the renaissance of ear diseases, Dr. Harold F. Schuknecht best embodied the ideal combination of clinical expertise and research, especially otopathology research and education. He trained hundreds of ear doctors who spread throughout the world. Those folks continued to contribute, not only to clinical care but to academic otology as well. For me and many of my peers, Schuknecht is like the trunk of a tree, with branches and leaves and seeds that go up and out and onward. Such is his influence on otology. Trained at the University of Chicago, the best ear research department of his day, he then went to Detroit, Michigan, and later became professor and chair of Harvard's Department of Otolaryngology Head and Neck Surgery and chief of otolaryngology at the Massachusetts Eye and Ear Infirmary in 1961. Doctors in the front row of Schuknecht's lectures might ask a question and be fearful of his response. I had the great privilege of being with him as a resident and staff member in Michigan and later in Boston.

Besides the giants of otology I've mentioned, many others contributed to the otology renaissance, only a few whom I mention now: Dr. George Shambaugh, professor of otolaryngology and department chair at Northwestern University; Dr. Fred R. Guilford from Houston, Texas, who introduced Thiersch grafts (to help mastoid surgery); Dr. Ben Senturia from Saint Louis, who studied otitis media; and Dr. Michel Portmann of France, who made multiple contributions. Dr. Dietrich Plester from Germany similarly made many contributions to clinical and surgical care of ear diseases, as did Dr. Howard House, the older brother of William House, who made most significant clinical contributions, especially regarding stapes surgery.

I, along with my colleagues at the Paparella Ear, Head and Neck Institute and the University of Minnesota, attempt to continue the great work of the leaders of the otology renaissance. Our practice has earned an international reputation for the treatment of ear conditions, and we have been devoted to patient care, education, and research in the Department of Otolaryngology at the University of Minnesota and previous universities. Our clinical and laboratory fellowship programs draw clinicians and researchers from across the globe. We continue to be devoted to conducting and furthering ear research. We recognize the great inheritance of the minds that came before us, and we're working hard to contribute to that lineage of excellence and innovation.

CHAPTER 1

The Miracle of
the Inner Ear

In normal development, around four weeks of human
gestation, embryonic cells of the eyes, nose, and inner
ears organize. Tiny pits appear on either side of the
fetus's neck. These depressions are the genesis of the
inner ear. Ossicles, at first a part of the fetus's jaw, harden
to bone, break away like icebergs off a glacier, float away
from the dentary bone, and become the hammer, anvil,
and stirrup of the middle ear. To form the external ear,
bulbous knobs, called hillocks, sprout and connect and
curl. As the face develops, the ear moves up the cranium
to positions lateral with the eyes. By twenty weeks, the
fetus, though swimming in amniotic fluid and saturated
with the noises of the inner workings of its mother's
heart and stomach, hears its first muffled sounds from
the world outside the womb. Near the end of gestation,
the human fetus can hear and react to the slamming of
a car door or the boom of a kick drum or the cooing of

its mother's voice. Unlike some other mammals, human offspring are born with their ear canals open. Upon emerging from the birth canal, the baby's ears capture his first unfiltered sound waves. The vibrating energy from the doctor's directions, the mother's cry, and the father's exclamations enter the infant's ear canals, vibrate the eardrums, and move the ossicles, the last of which, the stirrup, taps the cochlea, creating disturbances that move hairy structures called stereocilia, forcing a response from the hearing nerve and interpretation by the brain.

A cry in the night. Then a wail. Mom or Dad startle from sleep and rush to the nursery. There they discover a little one sitting in her crib, eyes wet, nose running, and her fingers tugging distinctively on her earlobe. The universal symbol for "Help me!" from a baby who hasn't yet said her first word.

Most parents, including me, remember the overwhelming sense of helplessness that comes when a baby gets an ear infection. The majority of children (95 percent) have at least one bout of otitis media before age five. Ear infections are a pain. They occur when swelling, a reaction from a cold or from allergies affecting Eustachian tubal function, prevents air from getting to the middle ear. That lack of air creates suction from the nose and throat, resulting in a lack of air in the middle ear, which introduces all kinds of germs from the Eustachian tube into an ideal breeding ground for bacteria and viruses. One-tenth of those children will experience some level of chronic hearing loss due to the persistent fluid buildup in the middle ear, otitis media with effusion. Sometimes this condition can lead to speaking delays.

Fortunately, the days of having to "wait it out," while the poor child "cries it out," are gone.

To enhance patient care, I developed new procedures and new tools to alleviate or cure diseases of the ear. For example, for children's ear infections, I designed three different types of ventilation tubes, made from silicon, that ameliorate the infant's disease and restore normal function and hearing. All over the world, people are walking around with my tubes in their ears. They're not a glamorous invention, but they've quietly improved the lives of thousands and thousands of moms and dads and babies. That makes me happy.

Sometimes, a child is born whose external and middle ear, usually for genetic reasons, has not fully developed and bone blocks sound energy from entering the ear canal. The fancy term for it is *congenital aural atresia*. The challenges of the corrective surgery for the condition are innumerable, but prominent among them is that common landmarks in the anatomy of the external and middle ear—which are normally used to figure out where to operate—simply aren't present. Cases like these are challenging. Microscopic surgery on the tiny ears of these children is akin to finding your way around on the surface of Mars. But, nothing is more rewarding than figuring it out, removing the bony blockage, and allowing the voices of Mom or Dad to enter the inner ear and do their dance. Then, the surprised smile of the child spreads from ear to ear. My heart leaps every time.

Humans use their sense of hearing to communicate, to feel pleasure, to be alerted, and to orient themselves in a changing environment. When my parents arrived in America from Italy, they didn't speak a word of English. They learned how to navigate their new lives by listening. I've spent my entire adult life studying the ear, researching diseases, inventing new tools, and developing new strategies and surgeries to help thousands and thousands of patients hear. I've been privileged to learn from giants in the field of otology, who resurrected the field after a long dormancy and who pushed me into leadership roles to further the study of pathology. For most of my career, I've also been a teacher, first as a staff member in Detroit and later as a faculty member at Harvard, Ohio State, and the University of Minnesota. Now my students practice otology in every corner of the globe.

For years, my family, friends, and students have been saying, "Paparella, you have to write that down!" or "Dad, write down that story about fixing up the soldier who had his ear bitten off by another soldier." Well, I've finally heard them.

So listen, and I'll tell you a story about how a poor kid from Detroit, just another son of an immigrant, no better than any other, came to have surgical instruments in his hands and who is still, in his senior years, revealing the world of sound to many patients a day.

CHAPTER 2

Beginnings, the Journey of an Immigrant

On February 13, 1933, my mother and father, Italian immigrants living on the east side of Detroit, Michigan, gazed down upon me, an infant in my mother's arms, deliberating over a name.

"George," said my father, "for the first president."

"Abraham," said my mother, *"per la sedicesima."* She knew President Lincoln's birthday was the day before mine. Thus, apparently, I could have been named Abraham Paparella. I'm sure that would have confused my friends.

Outside the walls of Harper Hospital, Detroit shivered with winter and economic uncertainty. Two of the largest banks in Michigan were on the verge of collapse. Henry Ford, the largest depositor of both banks, threatened to remove his assets. Just after midnight, in the early hours of my life, Governor William Comstock declared a banking holiday, which made it impossible to withdraw cash. What a man kept in his pocket or a woman had hidden in the flour container was all they had. My father, the only immigrant on our block who could read the English newspapers, awoke to headlines that read "Eight-day holiday for all banks in Michigan" and "Workers, make this the last depression!" and "Three thousand more join strike, demand pay raise and overtime."

My parents, hardworking but poor, welcomed me into the world in the middle of one of the worst economic depressions in history. One in four Detroit laborers was unemployed. The Ford Motor Company scrapped with its own workers who threatened to strike. The Mexican artist, Diego Rivera, painted the Detroit Industry Murals, a brilliant and damning set of frescoes depicting machines, including Ford's famous V8 engine, on the north and south walls of the Detroit Institute of Arts. *The Lone Ranger* debuted on WXYZ radio out of Detroit. FBI agents quietly patrolled the alleys and lanes in Detroit's Italian neighborhoods, where two Italian-language newspapers reported news from the homeland, as Benito Mussolini, prime minister of fascist Italy, dismantled democracy. On Brewster Street, a young Joe Louis was punching his way toward his first Golden Gloves win.

I was the fourth child of Vincenzo (Vincent) Paparella and Angiolina (Angelina) Creati. The fourth child to feed. The fourth to clothe. The fourth child they'd bring up to survive and thrive in America.

Ultimately, my father took a look at my head blanketed with the thick black hair of the Paparella line, sighed, and asked "Mauro?"

My mother shrugged and said, "*Perché no?*"

So Mauro I became, after my father's brother. (Years later, I changed my name to Michael Mauro Paparella, to be more American; I regret it.)

* * * * *

My father, Vincenzo, and his twin brother, Rocco, the sixth and seventh children of a brood that would total nine, were born in Corato, Italy, in September 1897 on a dirt-poor olive farm near the Adriatic Sea. While the region is beautiful—mountains, grapevines, and cherry orchards—life for my father's family was difficult, full of uncertainty and hardship, a concept he learned early.

Italy, as a country, was a relatively new experiment. The pope didn't trust the new government; the new government despised the pope. The north of the country seemed bent on industrialization. The south thought modern farming was the way to enter the new century. A king was assassinated. Bandits roamed the countryside. Mobs of criminals organized. Most people in the south were illiterate. There were earthquakes and crop failures. In the midst of all this chaos, my grandmother could no longer afford to keep my father. She cut his education short and fobbed him off on a merchant as a laborer. He was maybe nine or ten.

Even so, the merchant took pity on my father and took good care of him. My father learned the tile-making trade, and he was exposed to the opera. Through it all, he developed resilience, industriousness, and a lifelong love of music. Just as he was getting comfortable in his life with the merchant, his mother called him back. At the age of thirteen, he returned to work on the olive farm. His was a wretched childhood. His father was unable to provide for the family. His mother drank too much. She accused him of stealing, only discovering it wasn't true years later. It goes without saying that she beat him.

One and two and three at the time, my father's older siblings said *arrivederci* to life in Italy and immigrated to America. By the time he was seventeen, he had also skimped and saved for a ticket to America. He planned to set sail, with his brothers Mauro and Giovanni, to start a new adventure—first in Bristol, Connecticut, later in Berwick, Pennsylvania, the United States of America, where his oldest brother Michele, now Michael, lived.

My father traversed the ocean from Naples, Italy, to New York aboard the SS *Ancona*, an Italian passenger steamer carrying four hundred fifty souls. The Atlantic Ocean below the steamer hummed and ticked with the engines of German U-boats out on practice runs for what would soon erupt into the Great War.

He arrived at Ellis Island on April 7, 1914. Medical examiners checked him from head to toe—for lice, for rashes, for sores. They inspected his teeth, scrutinized his eyesight, and peered inside his ears. One flaw could get a man sorted into the "send back" line. Some Italians called Ellis Island *l'isola dell lagrime* (the island of tears) for this reason, along with the fact that the place was crawling with pickpockets and riffraff who would steal the laces out of your boots the minute you stepped off the boat if you weren't paying attention. Nevertheless, my father, bull-chested from his years of manual labor, passed the inspection and was pushed into Registry Hall, where there wasn't a name in the world the recorders couldn't botch. My father, Vincenzo, became Vincent. Good enough.

For a while Vincent and my uncles disappeared into the throngs of other Italian immigrants. There were so many of them and so many different immigrants that they didn't have to worry about learning English. Most employers didn't care if their employees could speak English. They only cared if they could work long hours without complaint. In fact, some employers preferred workers who couldn't speak English because employees who could all speak the same language were dangerous. They could share ideas and unite.

My father and his brothers spent some time building train cars at the American Car and Foundry Company in Berwick, Pennsylvania. But then they ended up where so many other southern Italians and other poor immigrants landed: in the most backbreaking and exploitative of industries, the Pennsylvania coal mines. They joined throngs of workers excavating the nation's electricity.

While working conditions were slowly improving, some would argue that they weren't improving fast enough. After a coal-worker strike a decade before, the federal government intervened and demanded that mining companies keep track of injuries on the job. Here's a short sample from a long list of persons with surnames beginning with "P" maimed and killed in 1914 in the mines of the Keystone State (from the Pennsylvania Historical and Museum Commission, Pennsylvania State Archives article "Mine Accident Registers 1907-1917"):

1914, Pacie, Augustine. 25, fatal, inside, laborer, Italian alien, fall of rock pillar work.

1914, Palmero, Joe. 67, fatal, inside, mason, Italian citizen, killed by cars.

1914, Petroskie, Peter. 27, nonfatal, inside, laborer, Polish alien, explosion of blast.

1914, Paploskie, Frank. 30, nonfatal, inside, miner, Russian alien, explosion of blast.

1914, Parker, Arthur. 33, nonfatal, inside, driver boss, American citizen, kicked by mule.

1914, Parry, Edward. 42, fatal, inside, miner, Welsh citizen, fall of roof at face.

1914, Passon, Angelo. 49, fatal, inside, miner, Italian citizen, fall of roof pillar work.

1914, Paul, Pasona. 22, nonfatal, inside, laborer, Italian alien, fall of roof in cross cut.

A few years passed this way, my father and his brothers avoiding death every day, three hundred feet below ground, so I doubt he even minded when he was required to register for the draft in June 1917. The Great War, World War I, was on.

My father reported to Camp Lee in Virginia on July 23, 1918. Knowing only a few words of English, most usefully, "yah," the army official handed him an apron, pointed in the direction of the mess hall, and relegated him to kitchen patrol.

He scrubbed pots and pans, picked stones out of buckets of dried beans, peeled thousands and thousands of spuds, ladled mush onto plates, mopped and polished floors gone dirty and dull by thousands of boot steps every day, and kept mice out of the food stores. All the while, my father listened. He never took a single class to learn English, but as he moved among those other young men, he listened to their talk of home; their stories of mothers, fathers, sisters, brothers, and sweethearts; their opinions of the war in Europe; their worries about the influenza pandemic sweeping the globe; and their frustrations over the spreading prohibition of beer and liquor. He listened to people reading aloud from newspapers, repeating President Wilson's position change from certain isolationism to stern condemnation to readying troops for deployment.

My father learned about the German U-boat that sank the RMS *Lusitania* carrying civilians. He learned about the German U-boat that torpedoed the SS *Ancona*, the very steamer that had carried him to New York, in the Mediterranean Sea. Two hundred and eight lives lost, most of them Italians trying to get to America. The twelve trunks of gold in the cargo, meant for purchasing arms, fell to the bottom of the sea, never to be recovered.

With enough English-language skills secured, my father was ordered to trade in his apron for an M1 carbine rifle, bayonet attached. On September 5, 1918, he and the rest of the fresh recruits of Company H of the 314th Infantry Regiment, 79th Division, American Expeditionary Force, lined up and boarded a ship to France and the Western Front, where the most intense battles of the Great War raged. Contradicting common sense, my father was lucky to be there because back at Camp Lee, an influenza outbreak swept through two weeks after his company was deployed, sickening twenty thousand soldiers and killing more than one thousand men.

On the front, the learning curve was steep. Once they landed, the young men of the 314th Infantry almost immediately boarded trains and rumbled past the smoldering ruins of villages, forests leveled to fields of spiked trunks, and blasted-out hillsides. When the train stopped, the young soldiers heard shelling and gunfire and, for the first time, the rolling tracks of tanks, machines they had only heard about, never seen. Here, they got their first glimpse of no-man's-land, a place completely devoid of all life. No trees. No grass. No insects. No rabbits. No birds. And, certainly, no men. Acres upon acres of death spread before my father's eyes. He was a few weeks shy of twenty years old. With the tinny scent of chemicals hanging in the air, down into the trenches they went. Into the earth like moles, they would eat, sleep, and fight for the next several months.

The Germans, who had been warring for four years by then, were well adjusted to trench warfare, but were nearing the end of their reserves. Old men had been pulled off their plows and young boys had been pulled away from their mother's skirts and sent to the front lines. By 1918, they were the face of the German offense. But they were good fighters—well trained and united in a way the United States Army, full of fresh immigrants, simply could not be.

The Americans had superior weaponry, but the soldiers weren't adept at using it. Back at Camp Lee, my father and the rest of his company had been trained in the ways of open warfare and aggressive offense. That training was not at all useful on the battlefields in the north of France. Tensions between General Pershing and the leaders of France and Britain, our allies, were high. Pershing had trained his troops the way he wanted and refused advice from the French and British. Once on the front, Pershing wouldn't mix his troops with theirs.

My father and his company barely captured the town of Malancourt on September 26. The next day, they met up with the 313th Infantry to take Montfaucon-d'Argonne from the Germans too. That battle was a chaotic bloodbath. There was so much smoke in the air that American and German soldiers stood elbow to elbow in no-man's-land, shooting in all directions. It took many days to account for the missing and the dead. After the 314th regrouped, along with the 313th, 315th, and 316th, they were charged with holding the line while the Germans shelled them by land and air and poisoned the air with mustard gas.

One day a bomb exploded near my father. Mud and shrapnel spiked through the air, and my father was hit in the stomach. He later said that at that moment, he entered a white tunnel and saw the face of God.

God was a busy greeter that day. Between September 26 and November 11, Armistice Day, twenty-six thousand American soldiers and more than twenty-eight thousand Germans died near the Argonne Forest. Luckily, God didn't want my father yet. He survived his white-tunnel experience and was back in America by the end of May 1919. Good thing for me.

My father didn't talk much about his war days. Records seem to suggest that after the war, for a time he went back to the dark and claustrophobic coal mines, where he would have grunted among the ear-splitting drills and clanging hammers, chisels, and falling rocks. Soon we find him again in Berwick, Pennsylvania— where, with the help of family members, he opened a dry goods and grocery store. As he made orders and organized shelves and served customers, he probably felt like he was becoming a real American. As he stood in the doorway of his shop and looked out at a changing world, he probably had a scrambled mess of scar tissue on his stomach and residual poison gas in his lungs. He probably still had coal dust under his fingernails and olive oil in the pores of skin. He was twenty-two. He was living the American dream.

Just one thing was missing: a wife.

CHAPTER 3

Foundations, the Making of an American Family

Picture my father behind the counter of his store in the small borough of Berwick, a place settled by Quakers, serious people who were dedicated to the temperance movement. But, if I knew my father (and I did), he's probably got a bottle of homemade wine, which he called dago red, behind the cans of Campbell's oxtail soup, Heinz spaghetti, and Van Camp's pork and beans on the shelves.

Berwick welcomes a swell of Slovak, Ukrainian, and Polish immigrants in the years after the Great War. Unlike the plain Quakers, the immigrant women wear colorful skirts, embroidered vests, and puff-sleeve blouses. The Polish men lumber about alone with long faces. They work hard, save their money, and then send for their families. Nearby, the American Car and Foundry Company churns out railroad freight cars and steel passenger cars. Also, just down the way, a grocer named Earl

Wise Sr. finds himself with too many potatoes and uses his mother's kitchen to make and bag what becomes known as potato chips. The small town of Berwick hosts a flurry of activity. Workers come in to my father's store to purchase coffee and sugar and bologna and canned peaches. Women wander in to buy flour and brooms, perhaps a hard candy for a child. These women recently earned the right to vote when the Nineteenth Amendment was ratified in August 1920. Their backs seem straighter. They speak a little louder.

At some point here, my grandfather, Filomeno, leaves Italy and winds up stuck at Ellis Island. The ship manifest shows that he had listed the wrong destination. Filomeno listed his son Mauro's former home in Niagara Falls as his destination. But Mauro was in Berwick with my father and his other brother. It's unclear whether Filomeno's sons knew their father was coming or not. In any case, he was released after three days. That is the last record of him anywhere until nearly two years later when my grandmother, Giuseppa, or Josephine, as she becomes known, is also stuck at Ellis Island. Records indicate she was held because she was illiterate, and it was noted that she had a "deformed hand" and was likely to become a "ward of the state." By this time, the United States Congress was putting the squeeze on new immigrants, inventing ways and passing laws to make it more and more difficult to get into the country. A few days later, my grandmother was released into the care of my grandfather.

Though my father rarely spoke of his parents, we know from family lore that Josephine spent at least some time with her sons in Berwick. The ship manifest tells us she had twenty-five dollars in her pocket when she arrived in America. She likely needed her sons' financial support. Nevertheless, it's possible that under her influence my father decided to become a proper married man.

Only a few years before, he had struck out on his own to the "brave new yonder" of the United States. He learned English. He became an American soldier, was wounded, and survived. He built a successful business in a nice American town. He was assimilating to his new life in this new place of modernization.

But, when it came time to pick a wife, my father returned to the old ways.

Traditionally, women made the matches, and Italians often married as a result of an exchange of letters and photographs with relatives acting as intermediaries. My father left his business in the care of his mother and other family members to once again traverse the ocean, so he could go to Italy and meet and marry his bride, sight unseen. A transatlantic crossing took just under five days.

On July 4, 1923, the birthday of the country, my father boarded the SS *Leviathan*. This passenger ship was built by the Germans and originally named the SS *Vaterland*, but the Americans took it from them during the Great War and never gave it back. They refurbished the innards in an Art Deco style and switched out the coal engines for oil burners. My father was on her maiden voyage as the *Leviathan*. Nelson Maples directed the ship's orchestra. Everyone's favorite tune was "Tell Me a Story," a foxtrot.

I like to imagine my father in a dark passenger area in his cot, stomach roiling. He was probably worried about his store, into which he'd poured so much time and money. He was probably nervous about meeting his fiancée. Would she find him handsome enough? Successful enough? Would she find him interesting? Could she cook? Was she pretty? No doubt his stomach also flipped and flopped from seasickness caused by the disconnected messages sent to his brain. One from the fluid in his inner ear telling his brain he was moving. The other from his body and eyes, telling his brain he was not. The relay of those two contradictory messages nauseates the healthiest man. I imagine he spent a lot of time pacing the deck, calming his nerves and settling his gut, perhaps being lulled by the SS *Leviathan* Orchestra.

My mother, Angiolina, was born near the Sangro River in the valley of the green Apennine Mountains in a village called Castel di Sangro, which means *castle of blood*. Her father, my grandfather, was the *capo di stazione*, the head of the train station, which was a very important job at that time as trains were the arteries that moved the agricultural goods and raw materials of southern Italy to the major cities and more industrialized north. The railroads were also unifying a country that had only recently been created after wars and annexes. Trains moved people, who moved culture and ideas through the mountains, over the rivers, and in between the olive groves.

My maternal grandfather raised his children with a stern focus on education for the boys, finding good husbands for his daughters, and a firm hand for all of them.

When the boys disobeyed, they'd be locked in the cellar as punishment for days on end. My grandmother, mother, and her sisters would weep silently into their handkerchiefs and secretly sneak food and water to the boys.

That was the way then. I have a large photo of my grandfather, Antonio Creati, in an oval wooden frame. In the photo, he's in his later years, with his carefully clipped white hair swept back. His face is round and open. Deep lines from his nose to his mouth hint at a smile. He's dressed sharply—black suit coat, black vest, and wide, silk tie. And his eyes, which remind me of my mother's, are smiling beneath large brows.

My mother was a vision of loveliness on her wedding day. Her first name means *angel*, and she looks like one. Her last name, Creati, means *creator* or *God*. She has short, black, bobbed hair with bangs, like the flapper girls of America did. Tulle from her veil rises around her head in a halo. In her right arm is a bouquet for the ages. It looks so heavy. With her left, she daintily manages the spray of gladiolas that fall from the bouquet all the way to the ground. My father, who stands proudly beside her, gently holds the lacy hem of her dress.

Once Vincent and Angiolina were married, they sailed for America, and just as Vincent had, Angiolina came through Ellis Island on December 19, 1923, and became Angelina. Upon their return, my parents wasted no time starting their family. My oldest sister, Josephine, was born in 1924. This should have been a happy time for them, but they soon discovered that while they had been getting acquainted and married in Italy, my father's mother had been busy ruining his business and reputation with bad dealings. The grocery and dry goods store that my father had worked so hard to build, that he depended upon to support his new family, was bust. Thus, my father made plans to escape his mother and venture off to find reliable work. All ears were on the Midwest, the beating heart of the industrial country. So that's where he turned his ears too.

CHAPTER 4

A Beautiful Boyhood in Detroit

Detroit. I'm hiding in a neighbor's tree, eating a stolen pear. Maybe I'm three or four years old. From here I can see the many houses on Zender Place. All the yards are dirt and gravel. Grass is for rich people. We aren't rich; no one here is. It seems like no one anywhere is rich.

Someone's mother is cooking sauerkraut. Yuck. Someone else's is cooking polenta. Yuck. From here, I can't smell what my mother is cooking. Sometimes she buys a live chicken from the eastern market and stabs a scissors down its beak into its throat. Feathers fly. After a while, the wings stop flapping and the legs stop kicking. Then she butchers and cooks the innards in boiling water, the white meat in a roasting pan, the dark meat in a skillet, and every part of it is delicious. There are sandwiches and sauces and soups for days.

My father is calling my childhood nickname. "Mowie! Mowie!"

I ignore him. I'm grinning widely. He asks my older brother, Tony, "Where is Mauro?" Tony shrugs. Pa asks my sisters, Josephine and Elsie. They know but don't tell. "It is time for dinner!" he shouts into the air. He asks the neighbors. Someone, a rat, points to the tree. My father spots me and loosens his belt. I stop smiling and drop from the limb. He's coming now. The faster he runs, the lower his pants fall. Soon his belt is in his hand, and his pants are on the ground. I dash home, giggling all the way. I fly through the door. The scene is reminiscent of a Fellini movie.

Mother is in the kitchen. She shakes her head at me, but her eyes are smiling. She turns up the heat on the stove. Live snails climb up the side of the fry pan but my mother scrapes them down, back into the splattering oil. When we gather at the table, my father, his anger forgotten, shovels the little gray creatures into his mouth. Olive oil drips from his lip. With a fork, I move a snail from one side of my plate to the other. It leaves a glossy trail.

"*Mangia!*" says Mother. She motions with her hand to eat. "*Mangia!*"

So I do.

Yuck.

* * * *

After my parents and their new daughter, Josephine, left Pennsylvania, they moved to Detroit, where my father took a job as a spot welder at Chrysler. In 1933, I was born, bringing their young family to six. Franklin

Delano Roosevelt was the new president. In Germany, Adolf Hitler came to power. This year was also the most difficult year of the Great Depression. My parents tried hard to be good Americans, as did so many of the other immigrants swarming Detroit at the time. Everyone was looking for a job. The population of Detroit swelled from 993,678 in 1920 to 1,568,662 in 1930. A quarter of the population was foreign-born.

My parents no doubt struggled and sometimes fought noisily with each other in the stress, but us kids didn't really feel it. Our parents sometimes argued, but so did everyone else's. We were poor, but so was everyone else.

While my mother had been raised to become a good wife and mother, both of which she was, she had to take a job in a factory. I often wonder what she thought of her life in America, if it was anything like she imagined it would be when my father was writing to her. The backdrop of her childhood was the natural beauty of the mountains, alongside a river, among ancient buildings. Imagine going from there to the middle of urban America in only a few short years, with a husband, with four children, and then a job in a car factory. Imagine doing all of that and still being poor. Sometimes, she stole toilet paper from the factory to bring home. I remember being embarrassed about that.

Still, she brought Italy with her. I can still taste, after all these years, her creamy cakes and nutty cookies and fruit pastries. She was an artist, and the kitchen was her studio.

Somehow, in 1941, my parents saved enough money to purchase a car: a basic Plymouth sedan. I thought we had hit the jackpot. At the age of eight, on a trip to visit relatives in Connecticut and New York, I sat between my mother and father in the front seat with my three siblings in the back. To my mind, I had the most responsible and important job in the world, staring intently out the front window and yelling "Stop sign!" or "Red light!" Of the many memorable moments on that trip, this one stands out the most: I met my grandmother Josephine, my father's mother. As family-oriented as my father was, he rarely spoke of his own parents or siblings. So I was surprised to learn that what looked like an itinerant woman begging strangers for money on a street corner in New York City was my grandmother. She needed a whiskey, she said.

My memory is a little slippery here. I believe we all went up to a small apartment, presumably where she lived. A man was passed out on the floor—Tony, I believe his name was. A cousin, perhaps? Anyway, I only remember swelling up with love for my father and wanting to get back in the car and drive away. This is the only memory I have of my grandmother.

I think that experience was when my siblings and I began to understand more clearly what he'd been through. He wanted us to have the childhood he didn't get to have. But he didn't want us to be spoiled either.

Our parents raised us to be helpful and industrious, and so, at about seven years old, I got my first job simonizing a car with old-fashioned hard wax. I applied a thin layer of wax to every nook and cranny, doorjamb and joint of that dull automobile and then delicately rubbed it off until the paint job shone. It took all day. I was paid fifty cents. In those days, a pound of oranges cost forty-nine cents. Ground beef cost about fifty cents a pound. Cream donuts were fifteen cents for a dozen, and a loaf of bread was ten or twelve cents.

Around that time, I was hired to paint advertising signs for the auto-parts store in our neighborhood. My knack for art extended to my grade school, where I was commissioned to paint posters and I entered my watercolors into a children's art contest. I won. A proud moment for me was walking through the Detroit Museum of Art, past the Rembrandts to the room that featured my own work.

"Pa," I said. "I'd like to be an artist."

He stared at my work. He was clearly proud of me. But with his hand that had tended olive trees, washed floors, shined boots, loaded rifles, mined coal, wiped counters, and welded metal, he squeezed my shoulder and said, "Shut up. You will be a doctor."

CHAPTER 5

Family and Music

Detroit. I'm ten or eleven. I'm practicing my trumpet. I have what they call a "good ear" for music. This instrument cost my family twelve dollars, which is a mighty sum. Nobody yells at me to stop the noise because I'm good and everybody likes the "G.I. Jive."

It's December, nearly Christmastime, but there is only a little snow on the ground. The snow is light and dusty and swirls around in the wind close to the ground until it settles in the sidewalk cracks or collects against trees. A skinny pine tree stands in the living room. We have no money for ornaments. But Josephine has a clever idea.

"Come on, Elsie," she says to my other sister. They put on coats, wrap scarves around their heads, and go outside.

I'm curious about what they're up to, but I must stay and practice my music. I won the all-city Detroit music competition for children. First place! I even have a little band. Last summer, we played a gig for the autoworkers' picnic when the regular orchestra didn't show up. We got paid even though we only knew six songs and just played them over and over. Mother and Pa also pay Mr. Peralta, who lives on East Grand Boulevard, to give me lessons. Going to his house is like passing through the gateway of heaven; it's so big and beautiful.

Mother is in the kitchen getting ready for Christmas dinner. A live turkey is in the kitchen too. It clucks nervously and gobbles like an out-of-tune horn.

"Tony!" she calls to my brother. *"Venire aiuto!"*

Because a turkey is a much larger bird than a chicken, two people are necessary to manage its demise. My big brother goes to help my mother. I hear the drawer where the scissors are kept being pulled open. I return to playing Johnny Mercer's song about the boys fighting overseas.

When Josephine and Elsie return, they ask Mother to use the scissors. Mother pauses while butchering the turkey and nods to where the scissors sit on the counter. Josephine rinses it off in the sink water and wipes it clean on a dishrag. Then Josephine and Elsie sit on the living room floor, near where I practice my trumpet. They pull dozens and dozens of silvery papers from their pockets. Foil from packs of cigarettes.

"We picked them up in the alley and on the street curb," Josephine says. She cuts them into thin strips, and Elsie hangs them from the needles of the tree. The thin metallic paper shimmers. Elsie stands back and squeals with delight.

"That looks good," Josephine says. "Play something festive," she tells me. She is my oldest sister and quite the boss, and I usually listen to her. I feel happy in our little house.

When Pa gets home, he shakes the snow off his coat and hat. He admires the tree and tells Mother that it smells good in here.

"Pa," I say. "When I grow up, I would like to be a musician."

He bops my head playfully. "Shut up. You're gonna be a doctor."

* * * * *

My early memories are filled with school days, bible camps, and neighborhood kids and family visitors. I was always a quick learner, had to be to keep up with my older siblings. At Harris Elementary School, I got bumped up two grades. I worked hard to keep up socially and academically, but it wasn't easy being the youngest boy in my class. My father talked endlessly of my education—that I'd go to college, that I'd be a doctor. I listened and absorbed his hopes for me.

My spiritual development was important to my parents, as well. Even though they'd both been devout Italian Catholics in Italy, America changed them a little bit. I'm not sure why, but I know anti-Catholic sentiment was strong in those years. In any case, while in Pennsylvania, my father converted and became a lay preacher in the Italian Gospel Hall, an offshoot of the Plymouth Brethren. The Protestant church was very strict: no dancing and no makeup, which would sometimes cause all sorts of problems between my sisters and mother. Once in a while, I'd be sent to bible camp in the Upper Peninsula of Michigan. My fellow campers and I were encouraged to sing "Jesus Loves Me" as loudly as possible, so Jesus would be sure to hear. The only thing that was certain for the Plymouth Brethren was that the rapture, the moment when God would collect the earth's true believers for heaven and destroy the rest of the world's population, was right around the corner.

Between that and the ongoing war, I was sure the world would end at any moment. Even before America entered World War II on December 7, 1941, after Japan bombed Pearl Harbor, Detroit was part of the war effort. Right after Christmas in 1940, during one of his fireside chats, President Roosevelt called on American factories to assist our allies in Europe. Detroit became the "arsenal of democracy." It seemed as if every factory in the city retooled for the war effort. The car factories modified operations to make amphibious jeeps, twenty-eight-ton tanks, and stratosphere antiaircraft guns. In Ford's Willow Run plant, workers ramped up production to ultimately make one B-24 Liberator bomber an hour. A vacuum cleaner factory began to produce gas masks instead.

So many men left for Europe—more than six hundred thousand from Michigan—that once again, the factories needed laborers. Women entered the workforce, and droves of people, a half million from the South, flooded Detroit and scooped up jobs. This migration caused enormous unrest. On the east side, where we lived with other immigrant families, the housing was scarce and generally subpar. But that's where the majority of the new wave of workers looked for housing and jobs. Some white workers and white communities disliked working and living alongside black workers. In June 1943, this sad and embarrassing reality came to a head in the Detroit race riot. My brother, a star trackster who attended a predominantly black school, was chased home with rocks. The rioting lasted for three days until President Roosevelt sent in the National Guard. Thirty-four people were killed. Twenty-five of them were black. My siblings and I just tried to stay out of the way and out of trouble during the riot and its aftermath.

Sports—basketball, football, and baseball—were a big thing in the neighborhood I grew up in, and they probably kept us boys from worrying our mothers too much. On the weekends, we'd gather at the athletic field, nothing but a patch of rocks and pebbles near Harris Elementary School. Because Detroit was so important to the armament of the Allied Forces, we all knew the entire city, including the schools, was a target. Even Joseph Stalin said, "Detroit is winning the war." School administrators and teachers regularly practiced air raid drills by teaching us to scramble under our desks, cower, and cover our heads with our hands. Would that have kept us safe if Hitler or Hirohito targeted the heart of the American military's weaponry-producing area? We didn't ask. Instead, out of school and free from worried parents, war concerns, and street violence, we'd organize ourselves into teams and play. Once in a while, though, the atmosphere of the day affected us and our teams behaved more like gangs. We got a little rough.

One day after a basketball game our team was walking down the sidewalk. Our captain, Butts deStilio, was up front. The team we'd just whipped was coming down the sidewalk in the opposite direction, led by their captain. Butts crossed his arms and widened his stance. The other captain did the same. The rest of the team members followed suit. Nobody budged, and it started to get a little tense. Butts told everybody that a fight would have to settle it. So, as a matter of pride and principle, we retreated into alleys and picked up broken bottles, boards with nails sticking out, hunks of broken cement, and rocks.

Until then, mostly our antics had been harmless, our trouble not too troublesome. We'd whistle at taxicabs and then run away once they stopped. We'd stare at street lamps as though something amazing were happening up there and get all the curious passersby to do so too. We stole pears and apples by climbing on the roofs of garages. Once a lady called the cops and an officer shot at us, probably just to scare us, but it did put a stop to our thievery for a while. With BB guns, we killed rats in the alleys and occasionally aimed at each other. I can still feel the sting. One time, we got into trouble for swimming across the Detroit River to get to Belle Isle. About three-quarters of the way across, we got in the way of a freighter, which seemed tall as a skyscraper from our vantage point. The Coast Guard came. Rather than pick us up out of the water and return us to shore, they made us turn around and swim back to Detroit. As I clawed my way out of that dirty water and onto the shore, I couldn't remember ever being so exhausted. It's a wonder nobody drowned.

Still, none of that was as scary as standing face to face with that rival gang. I wanted to run home, but I knew I couldn't. Finally, the leaders of our two gangs, after much twitching and a number of false starts, thought better of the situation and decided fighting wasn't wise. Our rival teams passed each other with some empty threats and trepidation, but with no harm done. If only the adults could have taken a lesson from us kids.

CHAPTER 6

In Times of War

The newspapers report there are five thousand WWII prisoners being held throughout Michigan. Sometimes, Mother and Pa host the Italian ones from Fort Wayne, which is situated on the Detroit River. Our German neighbors sometimes host German prisoners. The prisoners say nothing nice about Mussolini or Hitler— and not just because they crave a home-cooked meal from the Italians and Germans living in America. Most of them have been fighting in North Africa. Purple circles cup their eyes and long, deep wrinkles stretch across their foreheads, but the prisoners can barely grow whiskers on their lips. They are eighteen, nineteen, and twenty. They eat Mother's food with ferocity, so happy are they to taste the foods of home. Mother heaps ravioli and meatballs, hearty bread, soup with sausage, crusted chicken, and cake onto their plates. They seem like decent men, and some want to stay here after the war is over. They'd like to work in the factories that are currently building the war machinery and weapons being used by the Allies.

Once the war is over and the factories make cars again, the prisoners would like that very much.

Pa stares at our guests and then looks at Tony. If Pa had not gotten on that boat and moved to America, Tony could have shared these boys' plight. His son could be one of these prisoners. If the war doesn't end soon, I could've been one of these boys too.

The prisoners look a hundred years old. They whack their chests and cough. They rub their raw, red eyes. They lean forward and turn their heads so their good ears can hear the lively conversation. They don't say so, but I think they're all half deaf. The Detroit-made war machinery must be noisy while it blasts away at the Axis powers.

Meanwhile Josephine has graduated from Commerce High School. She works as a secretary at Packard Motor Company, which used to make luxury cars but now makes airplane engines. Her sweetheart and future husband, Ray, is part of the Normandy invasion and gets shot in his hand. Tony has graduated from Miller High School. He looks like Paul Newman in his Navy uniform. Elsie is still at Commerce High School. She wants to be a secretary at Packard too, but suitors are after her already, so who knows?

I'm soon to enter high school. Pa has done his research, and he says I'll attend Cass Technical High School located downtown. Cass Technical is the only college-preparatory school in Detroit. Only chosen students can attend.

"Quantitative chemistry!" he says. "Calculus! You will be a doctor. You will be a doctor. You will be a doctor."

Our entire Italian-American neighborhood has only one doctor, Dr. Gigante. He delivers the babies and takes out the tonsils and tends to the asthmatics and salves the rashes and stitches up the cuts. What do I know about any of those things?

I rub the scar on my finger. This past summer, Joe Altobelli, our pitcher and first basemen, threw me a drop curve, which missed my catcher's mitt and busted my finger. After the game, I stopped at the drugstore and bought a bandage. Then I used my good hand to straighten out the crooked finger and bind it tight. Everyone says Joe Altobelli will make it to the big leagues one day. Not as a pitcher, I think. But maybe if he sticks with first base, he will. My finger looks pretty good. Straight. If Pa has his way, maybe I'll be a big-league doctor. Later Joe became manager of the San Francisco Giants. He didn't like Candlestick Park and was fired. In 1983, he succeeded Earl Weaver as manager of the Baltimore Orioles, and in his first year, they won the World Series. Wow! Once when the Orioles played the Minnesota Twins, he came to my home for an Italian dinner. He left a brown bag behind with three balls signed by every member of the 1983 World Series Champions—a nice gift for each of my three kids.

* * * * *

While at Harris Elementary in eighth grade, I was elected class president. And, then in middle school at Barbara Intermediate, prodded along by some cute girls,

I ran again for office. Since I was now at a new school, I hardly knew anyone. I ran against two other boys who'd been attending Barbara Intermediate School for two years. The girls made "Vote for Paparella!" posters. They became my chorus as I traveled from homeroom to homeroom with my horn, playing "Hey! Ba-Ba-Re-Bop." We cleverly changed the words to "Hey, Paparella." Somehow, that won my classmates over, and I became the ninth-grade president. At the end of that year, my entire family attended the graduation exercises. Elsie slipped two fingers between her lips and whistled like a teakettle.

Even though I was only a year away from high school graduation at the ripe old age of fifteen, I continued to focus on music and sports. I joined the All-City Orchestra even though I wasn't very good at sight-reading music. I was a more of a play-it-by-ear kind of musician. Still, I got a few solos and did all right.

I also took up tennis. Why not? My buddy Myron and I easily became teammates on the Cass Tech Varsity Team; we played doubles and by hitting lobs most of the time won "All City." We heard that the Canadian Open was to be held in Windsor, Ontario, which is south of Detroit and accessible through the Ambassador Bridge over the Detroit River. Once we got there, we learned that we could sign up. So we did, mostly as a joke. In the first round, I played a fellow who was the husband of the number one–seeded female player. Having just driven down from Montreal, he was exhausted. And so I won.

My chest puffed up a bit.

The next round, for some reason, I drew a bye, which advanced me to the third round the next day. That evening Myron and I took in a movie in Windsor and saw a sports featurette about the two best American pros, Tony Trabert and Bill Talbert, playing doubles with the two best Canadian players, one of whom was named Henri Rochon.

The next day, we arrived early to check the schedule.

I ran my finger under my name: Mauro Paparella. I followed the connecting line to my opponent: Henri Rochon. My mouth went dry. My palms went sweaty. I read the rest of the information. Location: Main Stadium. Jackson Park. I knew fans paid a lot of money to attend. I felt hot, and I got dizzy.

"Myron," I said. "He's gonna kill me."

Myron nodded in agreement.

Before the match, Rochon stood coolly in front of a Ferrari with half a dozen beautiful girls looming about. He had dozens of tennis racquets and all kinds of equipment. Shaking on my knob-knees and holding my used tennis racquet, I felt like a kid getting ready for a beating. Was I nervous when the match started? You bet. But the fans, liking a good underdog story, rooted for me, especially when I tried to return Rochon's legacy shot, a drop shot. He, however, showed me no mercy. Amazingly, almost every game went to deuce. He won the first set 6–love, but in the first game of the second set, I managed an ace and won the first game. I wanted to throw my racquet in the air, rush back to Detroit, and fall into bed. Instead, I finished. Final score: 6–0, 6–1. Humiliation complete.

CHAPTER 7

A Young Man's Work

Josephine, Tony, and Elsie are out of the nest and making their own lives. It's quiet and a bit lonely. Too often, I can hear the clock ticking and floor creaking, noises I never noticed before. The house feels a bit darker and colder, but Mother and Pa lavish all their love and hopes on me.

Mother's hair is turning white, like her father's. She sweeps it to the back of her head, pins it at the nape of her neck. Sometimes, she talks of a headache and seems to stare too long out the window. Mother never complains, so I watch Pa for a reaction. Pa speaks to her in Italian and tells her she works too long and too hard and should lie down and take a rest. But, she doesn't. "*Deve studiare forte*," she says to me.

"I will, Mama," I say. Even though I'm years younger than my classmates, my grades are good. Already, I have a premed scholarship waiting for me at the University of Michigan. But first, I must finish my last year of high school.

I'm fifteen. I've never had a date.

To get to school, I hop a streetcar, then another, then a bus, and then I trek three blocks. I love the smell of the voltage and fuel in the air. The whole city seems electric, as if Detroit itself were a giant factory with moving parts.

But sometimes I can barely stay awake during class. I'm not tired, only bored. These classes, even the college-prep courses, are easy. I breeze by with little or no studying. Even though I hump books home and back to school again, I rarely open them unless Mother is watching me. I don't tell her about the number of school days I sneak out at lunch and head downtown to the cinema.

Abbott and Costello are kings of the screen. The 1947 comedy *Buck Privates Come Home* is my favorite. Herbie, who's played by Costello, cracks a joke that goes: "I'd rather marry a homely girl than a pretty girl anyway." Slicker, played by Abbott, asks "Why?" Herbie replies, "Homely girls are less likely to run away. And if they do, who cares?" That joke gets me every time.

After a film, I stop by Woolworth's dime store and buy an ice-cream sandwich, a slab of vanilla between two warm waffles. If there are pretty girls on the bus or streetcar home, I try not to drip. If there are homely girls around, I also try not to drip. But I think most girls are pretty. Much too pretty for me to talk to.

* * * * *

Life wasn't all movies and ice cream, of course. For as long as I can remember, I've had a job. From waxing cars and painting advertisements as a child, I moved up into factory work as a teenager during the summers.

For a while, I operated a punch press at Gemmer Steering Gear, where my pal Ken Afton also worked. Somehow, word got out that I was going to medical school.

"Hey, doctor, don't chop your fingers off!" the guys would tease.

I'd pretend I didn't know what they were talking about. They were a rough and rowdy bunch, many from the South, and I didn't want them to think I was some kind of wuss. I also worked at Chrysler Corporation and at Ford Motor Company for several summers. My job at Chrysler was in the final car-assembly line, where I attached backup lights and bumper brackets. After a full day working in "the pit," I'd collect thick tar on my boots and go home one or two inches taller.

"*Il pavimento!*" my mother would shriek, pointing at my boots and her rugs.

Later, there was an opening at the United States Rubber Company, later known as Uniroyal, in research and development. Even though I wasn't the best student all the time, my mind was hungry and curious, so I applied and got the job. U.S. Rubber manufactured tires for cars, trucks, and airplanes. I prepared myself to be in a lab coat with a clipboard, taking notes. Instead, I was the man who had to climb up big, dirty machines to change tires that had been subjected to all kinds of tests: how they fared in cold or hot weather, how they fared on cement, tar, gravel, or greasy surfaces.

My chest began to expand to the girth of my father's. Finally, I was promoted to the dynamometer room. Boy, I thought I'd made it then! But being lowest on the totem pole, my shift went from midnight to 8:00 a.m. During those hours, I "landed" airplane tires, twice as tall as me, against a rotating metal wheel to simulate and test the durability of the rubber under various conditions. Sometimes I'd get tired and find myself watching the current of the Detroit River. Its darkness struck me as very melancholy at four and five o'clock in the morning.

Then Ken thought the two of us should get jobs at Pfeiffer Brewing Company. I couldn't disagree with the logic of that. We were hired as what they called "soakers." Two of us sat on opposite sides of an automated line. Using hooks, we'd open each returned case of beer bottles (a case had twenty-four bottles), and we'd throw out the bad bottles that couldn't be washed and reused. You don't want to know some of the disgusting things people stick into beer bottles.

From there, the bottles moved onto a gold-chained platform for sterilization before they went to the filler. After that came pasteurization and capping. Finally, the bottles of beer flew through a lighted box, where it was our job to spot any with impurities in the beer.

Yeah, right.

I still get dizzy thinking about it. Lots of the guys got nystagmus, where your eyes move uncontrollably and involuntarily back and forth.

Imagine driving home.

Speaking of that.

We were allowed to drink as much beer as we liked while working. We always drank the cold, unpasteurized stuff because it tasted the best. I didn't typically overindulge, but I sure worked with some guys who did. Five old-timers, veterans of the job, routinely consumed two cases each in an eight hour shift. And on Fridays, after they picked up their paychecks, they'd head to the bar across the street to hit the hard stuff.

I began to look up to these guys, and I guess I wanted their approval. One shift, I drank an entire case myself. On the way home, I drove onto a couple of lawns, knocked down a small tree, and took out a few mailboxes. I was lucky to not be stopped by the cops—and lucky to not kill anybody. I never did that again.

CHAPTER 8

College and Cars

Tony and I are the only two guys from our neighborhood to go to college. Tony's on the GI Bill and is going to be a bigwig architect. Most everybody else is staying in the factories—except Joe Altobelli, who's off to the Major Leagues (as a first basemen, thank God), and a couple of our pals who are already in jail for stealing and fighting, stuff like that.

It is 1950. I'm sixteen and at the University of Michigan. Ann Arbor is forty miles from Detroit, but it may as well be on the other side of the world. Instead of staying in my dorm room and studying, I spend too much time driving back and forth in my parents' old Plymouth. I want to see my mother, but I don't want her to come to Ann Arbor.

Her English is terrible. She wears old, dark, and drab European clothing. She is poor. And she looks nothing like the mothers of the other students. Their mothers have fashionable hair, artfully shaped and held in place with spray. Their colorful dresses spin when they turn and their pumps have skinny heels. They speak perfect English through red or pink lips. Some of them smoke cigarettes. Many of them look young enough to be sisters rather than mothers. They've never worked a day in a car factory. My mother's hair grows more and more white. I have an urgent desire to see her and be near her although I can't identify exactly why.

I hold my midterm grades in my hands, the first real grades I earned in my first year at the University of Michigan. Three Ds and a C stare back at me in cold, hard ink. It seems impossible. I've never seen grades like these. Never. My father's voice pops into my mind: "Mauro, you will be a doctor."

"Paparella, let me see," one of my classmates says. He peers over my shoulder. It's too late to hide the evidence. "Oh, man," he scoffs. He snatches the paper to take a closer look. "You're dreaming, Paparella, if you think that's going to get you into medical school." He hands me back my midterms and put his hand on my shoulder. "You need all A's." He raises one eyebrow. "All A's."

I exhale. "I know." I drag my feet to German class. The weight of my father's expectations and my own disappointment hang like an engine block from my neck. Maybe I'm not cut out for college. Maybe I should've stayed in the factory, sanitizing beer bottles or spinning tires. I sulk in my seat at the back of the room and daydream for a half hour.

"Mauro!" the professor roars.

When I look up, the entire class has turned around and is staring at me. They snicker. My face gets hot. "Me?" I ask.

The professor looks at me like: *Are you stupid? Of course you.* "I want to see you after class."

I nod. A couple of other students shake their heads and roll their eyes at me as though I'm the biggest idiot to ever walk the halls of this school. Maybe the professor will kill me and put me out of my misery.

After class, I trudge to his office. My stomach flops like a fish. I gingerly rap on the door.

"Come in, Mauro. Sit down."

Rather than his blustery, stern classroom demeanor, in his office the professor is quieter and kindly. He folds his hands on top of his desk.

"You have to work harder," he says. "You don't and won't ever have the advantages of the other young men in this university."

I stare at my worn boots, the boots of a welder's son. They aren't anything like the slim-laced oxfords and sleek slip-on loafers of my classmates from the East Coast.

"Do you understand what I'm telling you?"

I nod.

"You have a sharp mind, but now is the time you must work at your studies." He pauses a moment with the drama of a German. "You have developed bad study habits," he declares. He hardly knows me, but he is right.

I open my mouth. Close it again. In my mind rumble a million defenses about my work ethic, about how I've been working since I was seven years old. But the words don't form. And they don't have to.

He puts up his hand and then jabs a finger on a textbook. "*This* kind of work is important now."

I nod again and get ready to leave his office.

He leans back in his chair again. "I love so many languages," he says wistfully.

Germans are so strange, I think.

"But, the Italian language is one of the most beautiful in the world."

Germans are hard as steel one moment, but on the verge of silly romanticism the next.

He crosses his arms. "So musical and alive. So much rhyme and passion."

I think about my mother and brighten.

He slaps a hand on his leg. "Do you know the ugliest?" He has hardened again.

I shake my head no.

"It's Americans trying to speak German. It should be a crime." He waves his hand at me. "You may go."

I feel lighter as I walk to the Plymouth. I throw my books in the car, though not as violently as I usually do. Even though it's late, I decide to go home, if only for a night. I get in and drive. It's warm, and I feel better. The miles of passing darkness lull me into a deep, comfortable fatigue. I close my eyes until I hear the tires rattling and feel the steering wheel pull on the gravel. I snap awake and drive a few more miles until my eyelids droop again. I'm older now and should be more responsible, I tell myself. I pull over to grab a quick nap. I rest my head on my textbooks. Just a snooze, I think, before I doze off into a fitful sleep.

In my dream, a monstrous thundercloud is coming at me. It stabs at me with lightning and blows in with tornado winds. I jolt awake and sit straight up in the car. The car is moving, being lifted slightly up and down, in the back draft of a roaring freight train. I have unknowingly parked a few feet from a railroad track.

* * * * *

By the end of that semester, I had recovered and earned two A's and two B's. While my study habits never approached perfect, they did improve. After a year and a half in university housing, I was recruited, pledged, and entered Phi Kappa Sigma (PKS); probably because even though I wasn't very adept at making new friends, I developed a band that often appeared at the university's special events, football games, pep fests, and fraternity parties around Ann Arbor. I believe we were the first pep band in the stands before the university marching band. People got to know my face and must have assumed I was somebody.

Part of my pledge consisted of being blindfolded and taken to a rural area outside of town. I had to figure out how to get back, which was a bit scary since I was a city kid unaccustomed to being out in wide, open spaces. Where were the lights? The streetcars? The cars? The buildings? All I smelled was cow manure and sawdust. But I figured it out.

Back then PKS was one of the smaller fraternities, but the fraternity house had the largest bar in Ann Arbor, which drew a lot of people. That, and the fact that some of the best football players lived there, including the star halfback Tony Branoff, even though Bennie Oosterbaan, head coach of the Wolverines, kept Tony on a short leash.

I had three assigned jobs in the fraternity: one was to paint a huge mural behind the bar; the second was to take care of Kapper, the fraternity's mascot; and I was director of the glee club.

I wish the house still stood. Unfortunately, it was taken down and with it went my beautiful mural of voluptuous naked ladies behind the bar where we'd sit to drink beer and gaze.

"You shoulda made her hips bigger," one guy complained.

"Nah," another would say. "They're perfect."

Kapper, a dachshund, was a handful, a bit horny and always naughty. He chased bigger dogs and humped them shamelessly. He was also fond of knocking over and eating out of the garbage cans, a habit that made a lot of our neighbors angry. When we had school vacations and breaks, I had to take him home to Detroit, where he ate my mother's leftover meatballs and spaghetti right from the table. He loved that.

My mother, not so much. *"Cane sporco!"*

Kapper would hustle outside when my mother raised her voice or her spoon.

Under my leadership, the PKS glee club was democratic, very American—anyone could participate. The audition consisted of singing "Twinkle, Twinkle, Little Star." Five members were either deaf or monotone, so I placed them in the back.

"Softer, softer," I said when they howled like wolves. We sang at parties, but our specialty was appearing outside the girls' dorm rooms and crooning "I Love You Truly" in our corniest, best effort to impress them.

I was young, younger than my fellow students, and a few years make a big difference in early adulthood. But I was finding ways to make friends and fit in. Soon I wasn't making quite so many trips home to visit my mother.

The fraternity was a place of great diversity. Three of my closest friends were Puerto Rican. José Correa's dad was a professor at the University of Puerto Rico. Louie Rodrigues's uncle was governor of Puerto Rico. And then there was Frank Delgado, the resident ladies' man. Those three invited Tony Branoff and me to Puerto Rico.

I was scared to death.

I had never been out of state alone, much less the country. But I said, "Yes, let's go."

Coach Oosterbaan told Tony, "Hell no! You'll catch syphilis if you go down there," so he ended up ducking out of the trip. He stayed home nursing a cartilage injury he'd sustained in high school. That knee would haunt him later.

Woody Denton, a fraternity brother of ours, decided to come instead. Later, he would become a dentist.

The first night we were there, we were taken to the China Doll, an active nightclub with illegal gambling going on. Police cars zoomed on site; officers raided the club, captured us, and we were brought to court before a blind judge. What would my mother think, I wondered. This blind judge sympathized with our plight. We were college students. Just having a good time. Not causing any trouble. Yada, yada. My Puerto Rican friends made our case. The judge released us, and we didn't have to go to jail. Undeterred by that courtroom detour, Frank, José, and Louie wanted to hit up a whorehouse.

"No way," I said.

The rest of the trip went off without a hitch. Felisa Rincón de Gautier, the famous mayor of San Juan and a relative of José's, threw us a lavish party, like one you might see in a Hollywood movie. In San Juan, while sunning in Jose's backyard, I saw miniature "dinosaurs," which scared the hell out of me. They were just innocent geckos, but I had no idea such a creature existed. I drank and grew emboldened enough to argue art with José's dad, a professor of dermatology at the University of Puerto Rico.

"Modern art," I asserted, "is the medium of the people."

"Modern art," he said, "lacks historical perspective."

We swam in the ocean. The only water I'd ever swum in before was the industrial waste dump of the cold, fresh-watered Detroit River. I'd never been held buoyant by salt water. I inhaled deeply and let my chest hold me afloat with barely an effort at all. I never wondered about my parents, who had grown up next to such waters and who hadn't seen or smelled or felt them in decades. I just opened my arms and floated.

Later that night, I held a woman in my arms for the first time. An old woman with an enormous mansion hosted a party and music. Sugarcane workers who labored all day in the fields made up the band. By now, my ear was pitch-perfect, and I knew the music they made on that perfect night was perfect too. My legs and arms wanted to move and so I danced with a pretty girl in my arms.

The girls' chaperones removed themselves to a party in the back. I drank rum cocktails with fruits I'd never seen and worked up my conviction. I danced with one girl, then another. They smelled of salt water and sea air. They taught me the rumba, the mambo, the samba, and the merengue. And I have never forgotten.

As we boarded the plane to head back to Michigan, I was full of joy and confidence and resolve. Entering the plane, I shouted down to José's dad, "Modern art is here to stay!"

I felt as though my life were just beginning.

When I returned to Ann Arbor, I received a message: *Mother is very sick. Come home.*

CHAPTER 9

A Difficult Good-Bye

Detroit, May 1952. Pa paces the house, looking for something to do. He sneaks outside and hides behind the garage to smoke a cigarette. He thinks I don't know. My mother sits in a chair, her legs covered with a handmade blanket, its pattern a linked collection of starburst shapes. At her feet sits an old pail, in case she vomits. But she eats nothing anymore.

"Mama?" I ask. "Are you warm enough?"

Pa comes back in and turns up the radio. Virgil Trucks, pitcher of the Detroit Tigers, is in the midst of a no-hitter against the Washington Senators; it's the top of the eighth, and the score is 0–0.

"Trucks used to be a Navy boy," the announcer says.

"Like Tony," Pa says.

I nod and tuck the blanket more securely around Mother's waist. "Cold?" I ask.

Pa opens the refrigerator. It's stuffed with pots and pans and bowls of leftovers. My sisters have been bring-ing food that would require ten people plus all of their descendants to finish. Even so, Pa is getting skinny. If Mother were lucid, she'd be worried about his gaunt cheeks. She wouldn't be happy with how his shirt is draping off his shoulders. "*Mangia!*" she'd shout.

Pa removes a sausage, unwraps the butcher paper, and slices off a thin piece.

"Tigers better score some runs," the radio announcer says.

Pa puts the meat in his mouth and chews absent-mindedly.

Mother looks at me as though she's trying to place me. One side of her face seems stuck in a frozen grimace. Her white hair, still thick, is freshly washed and damp.

Pa pours a tiny bit of wine into a glass and brings it to Mother. He holds a napkin under her chin as he lifts the glass to her lips. "That will warm you up, won't it!" he says to her. She sips a little. He kisses her forehead at her hairline. Her eyes watch his every move. She trusts him.

The Tigers don't score in the bottom of the eighth. Trucks holds the Senators in the top of the ninth.

Behind her eyes, a tumor grows in the white matter of Mother's brain. It might be the size of a lemon, maybe an orange.

Dr. Gurdgeon, the neurosurgeon I found, is a good man. He's a professor from Wayne State University. He tells me that the glial cells, the star-shaped astrocytes responsible for the health of brain neurons, are growing uncontrolled. In normal function, these starry cells make imagination and creativity possible. They insulate and inspire and modulate neural activity. Without them, the neurons would do nothing more than react reflexively. My mother's glial cells refuse to be contained. They will grow and expand and spread. The cranium is a small place. The pressure will continue to cause headaches and nausea and vomiting. She will forget more and more. She will lose more mobility. A powerful drowsiness will overcome her. She will struggle to breathe. She will lose consciousness.

The tumor, a glioblastoma multiforme, will kill her.

Dr. Gurdgeon tells me all of this because I'm a premed student, so presumably I'm the person who can interpret and deliver this information to the rest of the family. I'm premed because Pa said, over and over, "Shut up. You will be a doctor."

I try. I do my best. I'm nineteen.

I translate what Dr. Gurdgeon tells me to Pa and Tony and Josephine and Elsie. "Mama has a malignant brain tumor that is growing very quickly. There's no stopping it. We must make her as comfortable as possible and tell her we love her."

So that's what we do.

"Last chance," the radio announcer says.

I pull out a chair and sit and listen to the game with my father, even though I know he's not listening. In the bottom of the ninth, the Tigers' right fielder Vic Wertz crushes a homer.

"It's gone!" the announcer cheers.

"That's good, isn't it, Mama?" Pa says.

My mother darts her eyes to him. They're wet with tears. She dies within a few days.

* * * * *

After my undergraduate premed courses, I applied and was readily accepted to the University of Michigan Medical School, after only three and a half years. I applied to no others. It was a good school, of course, but I wanted to stay close to my father. Every day I wondered who would take care of him with my mother gone. I didn't move back in with him, though. He was already wondering why it was taking me so long to finish school and get "a real job." Pa wanted me to be a doctor, sure, but he didn't understand what that entailed. So, instead, I rented a room in Ann Arbor from an elderly woman.

Maybe I was distracted, or maybe I was still just a bad student, but my study habits left a lot to be desired again. My father continued to say, "You will be a doctor." If I expressed any doubt about my abilities, he'd always say, "Get there first. Be the first to show up."

Just be the first to show up to what? Apparently he thought I could hurry the process along.

I went to most of my classes. I slinked in and slid along the wall to the back row and slouched down in a desk. Never raised my hand. Never asked questions. If I had a test, I'd avoid studying until the very last minute.

Say the test was on Thursday. On Monday, I'd remind myself about the test and then head to the Flame Show Bar in Ann Arbor and shoot pool. On Tuesday, I'd write, "Test on Thursday" on a notepad—and then head out to the Flame Show Bar to shoot pool. On Wednesday, I'd make coffee, read my reminder about the test, and arrange my books and notebooks. I'd drink the coffee, and then head out to the Flame Show Bar to shoot pool. Eventually I'd go home, open the textbook, listen to the binding crack, and smell the distinctive "new book" scent. Then I'd skim ten or twelve chapters in an all-night binge, fall asleep at the table, and wake again in time to leave for the test in a fog.

Eventually, the classes became more hands-on and my insecurity and inefficiencies were more difficult to hide. One day I was studying a slice of brain under the microscope in neuroanatomy lab, which was taught by a famous professor of neuroanatomy, Elizabeth C. "Ma" Crosby. She was the first woman to earn a full professorship at the University of Michigan Medical School. She specialized in the study of reptilian nervous systems. Her thesis was titled "The Forebrain of Alligator Mississippiensis," and all the brown-nosing students had read it. I, of course, had not. Professor Crosby was short and had one of those hard-to-read thin mouths—was it smiling or was it tense in displeasure?

She was brilliant, but she hardly said a word. I was scared of her. As I squinted at my brain sample under the microscope, I knew I had to work up the courage to ask her a question. Glial cells, astrocytes, I could see. The stars. Just like the ones that had smothered my mother's brain.

But, what was the rest of this stuff? What had Dr. Gurdgeon said? What had Professor Crosby said?

I timidly raised my hand. Only as high as my face. Over she came. She listened attentively to my question and then began to explain the sample to me, personally. This instruction was different than what I'd grown used to. Professor Crosby relaxed and became conversational about the brain matter. First one classmate came over, and then another. And, soon, there were so many classmates at my station that I was pushed out of the way—and out of the answer to my own question. I tiptoed from the periphery and could barely make out the top of her head.

Professor Crosby went on to win many awards, including the National Medal of Science, awarded to her by Jimmy Carter in 1979. Her studies of reptilian nervous systems contributed to the continued understanding of evolution. She researched and taught well into her nineties; that's a lesson I may have taken to heart, even if I didn't know it at the time.

I decided to move out of the room I was renting from the elderly lady because she was a snoop. She'd come up with all kinds of excuses to clean under my bed and would regularly put my shoes on top of my blankets. Finally, I began bringing the skeletons of feet home from school and arranging them in those shoes. She stopped touching my shoes. Still, I had to get out of there. I became a member of the Alpha Kappa Kappa medical fraternity. While I could have moved into the Alpha Kappa Kappa house, I decided to rent an apartment with a couple of buddies—one of them, Roland Hiss, was the cymbal player in the marching band.

He practiced and practiced and practiced. *Crash.* There fell a picture from the wall. *Crash.* There went a glass off the table. *Crash.* There went my last nerve.

After days like this, another friend, Ken Andrezejew-ski, would have pity on us and invite us to his dad's place on East Outer Drive where there was always a party going on. High class. Ken's dad was a successful lawyer. His parties usually featured records of Stan Kenton's futuristic jazz band. Kenton was the last of the big innovative band generation of the 1930s and 1940s, and he was in Detroit trying to form a new band and talking all the time about jazz education for children. Kenton's compositions were innovative and dangerous—and always, always loud. It was at one of these parties that I looked across a room and saw Lynne Behlow, who was looking right back at me.

Maybe it was the music, or maybe a memory of Puerto Rico, or maybe the loss of my mother, or maybe the few drinks I'd had, or maybe my father in my head saying "Get there first," but I dropped my insecurities and went up to her.

I don't remember what I said at first. But, I guess it doesn't matter. I was in love for the first time in my life and decided I was going to marry her.

The rest of the night we were inseparable. She told me she was a telephone operator at Bell Telephone Company. I told her I had a band. She cocked an eyebrow, looking simultaneously suspicious and unimpressed. So I told her I was going to be a doctor.

"What kind of doctor?"

Good question.

CHAPTER 10

Peering into Ears

It's 1956, and I'm twenty-three. I marry that beautiful telephone operator. I'm still a medical student, but I deliver the babies and tend the asthmatics and salve the rashes and stitch up the cuts, just as old Dr. Gigante, the family general practitioner, did (locum tenens). I know a little bit about just about every ache and pain and injury that walks through the door. I feel people's swollen glands and shine lights up their noses and swab the backs of their throats.

Droves and droves of mothers at the ends of their wits, holding wailing babies pulling on their ears, visit me.

Earache pain is real; it can feel hot or dull or sharp. The pain can occur at the source or it can hurt in the jaw, the temple, the eyes, or the sinuses.

"Where does it hurt?" I ask the children. Sometimes they point at their heads, sometimes they bury them in their mother's necks, and sometimes they just say, "In my ear."

"We're going to fix you up," I tell them. I gently examine their ears and noses and throats to make the proper diagnosis and prescribe the correct course of action.

Often the child has fallen asleep by the end of the examination, and the mother looks at me with pure gratitude.

I see a lot of old men who are losing their hearing. They're usually embarrassed, as though losing their hearing were a character flaw. Losing their hearing affects every aspect of their lives. They worry they can't drive. They worry they'll lose their jobs. They worry they won't be able to communicate with their families. As I gaze inside their ears, alighting the red swollen eardrum (tympanic membrane), a diagnosis and treatment is made. Their quality of life will not suffer.

Soon my mind turns over and over with questions about what, exactly, causes otitis media in children? What, exactly, causes deafness in the elderly? Rather than simply treating the symptoms, I begin to wonder if we know what we need to know to prevent them in the first place.

I decide I like ear, nose, and throat practice, a study that's called otolaryngology, which no one can pronounce. Paparella, the otolaryngologist. I grab myself an internship in Oregon, and after that I'll have a residency right back at the Henry Ford Hospital in Detroit.

For right now, though, I'm making money.

I splurge on a car in 1957, the first major purchase of my life. It's a svelte, golden Plymouth with wings in the back and taillights like dragon eyes. I cruise it back to Zender Place and park in front of the old house. I see the curtain pull back and Pa wave. I wave back, grab my keys, and go inside. It smells like burnt grease and like the garbage needs to be taken out.

"Pa," I say. "What do you think of my car?" I jingle the keys.

He glances out the window again. "Very nice," he says. "You graduate yet?" he asks. "Time to get a real job." He holds up a meatball that's singed on one side and looks raw on the other. "Want one?"

"Soon, Pa. Medical school takes time." I shake my head at his forkful. "You need a wife."

"What?" He stuffs the entire ball into his mouth. Chews a bit. "You think my food is no good?"

My brother has his own life. Josephine, hers. And kids! Elsie has her own too. We all do our best for our father, but he's an aging Italian man. That's the way it is. Like an old dog, he's not likely to learn new tricks. The dishes, caked with food from days ago, sit in the sink.

I drum my fingers on the table. "Pa," I say. "I—Lynne and I—have to move to Oregon."

"Oh," he says. "And then you'll get a regular job?"

"An internship is like a job," I tell him.

"Is it full time?"

"We're leaving soon."

"You go on," he says. "I hear it always rains there." His clothes are stained. He needs to shave. "I made wine." He rubs his scruffy chin. He coughs.

"You should quit smoking," I tell him. "I'd feel better about leaving if you had someone here to help you."

"Mind your own business," he says. "You may be a doctor, but I'm still the father."

"All right," I say. Stubborn old man, I think. I stand. "Come on. Come and sit in the car and listen to the radio with me."

John Coltrane, Ella Fitzgerald, Nat King Cole, Stan Kenton, Peggy Lee, Glen Campbell, Doris Day, Patsy Cline, and a newcomer named Johnny Cash. Pa pats his hand on his thigh along with the beat. Chuck Berry's "Roll Over Beethoven" rolls over the airwaves.

Pa taps his foot. Pa's got good rhythm. "I don't smoke," he insists as he stares out the window at the empty house with his yellow fingers.

* * * * *

Our senses of touch and hearing rely on vibrations to stimulate nerves and interpretation by the brain. The relationship between touch and hearing is so entwined that some researchers think the ear developed out of an embryonic skin organ as a high-functioning frequency receptor. Consider how a lullaby physically calms a baby. Think about how a rhythmic song inspires a body to dance. A diminished ability to hear, interestingly, can be related to a diminished ability to feel.

Music, one of my lifelong passions, is a controlled movement of sound waves. If I blow a note on my trumpet, say, the force of my breath through the instrument forces air particles to move through space. This disturbance creates a vibration, which makes a sound. If I play my instrument well (and I try), my ear recognizes patterns, detects frequency, and hears pitch.

The outer ear, called the pinna, that strange combination of cartilage and skin, has evolved to capture waves, funnel them to the middle ear for filtration and amplification through the middle ear, and then on to the inner ear, which creates electrical impulses that are sent on to the brain via the auditory nerve for interpretation. The outer ear also helps us figure out where sound is coming from. The pinnae have developed to best capture pitches in the range of the human voice. Animals tend to have higher developed pinnae for this function.

Early in my third year as a medical student I had no idea what kind of doctor I was to become. At that time I had two jobs. I had a band that played musical gigs three or more times a week. We were especially popular at high school proms and the Hillel House in Ann Arbor. I also worked as an extern performing histories and physicals at St. Joseph's Hospital, where the medical school faculty cared for private patients.

For a time, I was also an extern at a nearby psychiatric hospital, again doing histories and physicals. In the late 1930s, Julius Lempert, a giant in the history of otology, created the first one-stage operation that cured deafness in many patients with otosclerosis. Symptoms can drive patients crazy. There's sometimes tinnitus, head noise, like ringing and buzzing, associated with hearing loss. Lempert's nephew, Irving Blatt, a resident at the University of Michigan, was doing mastoid surgical operations for chronic otitis media (middle-ear infections) and chronic mastoiditis (chronic infection of the mastoid bone) at that same psychiatric hospital.

Every chance I got, I'd watch Blatt work. For the five or more hours of the operation, he'd be swearing and yelling up a storm. His instruments and bone-chips flew around the operating room. The nurses and I ducked and dipped. Despite what I considered to be a horrifying experience watching him, I was intrigued by his success and the delicate work of otology.

I was especially impressed by the speedy recovery of his patients. Surprisingly, even after what looked like brutal operations, the patients awoke smiling and happy, and they recovered quickly. The same was true in patients who had tonsillectomies, operations on the nasal septum, or other ear, neck, or throat procedures. The patients came in for their operations and left in great spirits after a brief stay. In contrast, I'd noticed in my other work and hospital rounds that patients with neurological, neurosurgical, and general surgical problems were much sicker and stayed in the hospital a long time, with a heavy cloud of depression surrounding their comings and goings.

I began skipping classes (again) during my third year of medical school to make regular trips to visit with an up-and-coming doctor by the name of Harold Schuknecht in Detroit. He was a tall, formidable presence, the son of a German immigrant farmer, and many people were afraid of his authoritative manner. He'd recently transferred from the University of Chicago, then thought to have the strongest research department in the United States, to Henry Ford Hospital. I'd watch him in his laboratory while he stared into a microscope, studying the hair cells of the organ of Corti in the cochlea. The hair cells amplify sound waves and then send sound information to the brain for interpretation. Tiny vestibular sensory receptors are also responsible for a human's sense of balance. Decibels louder than ninety will temporarily flatten the cells, causing temporary hearing loss. Long-term exposure to loud noise, some diseases, or aging can kill the hair cells, which leads to permanent hearing loss. Schuknecht, a big guy with a big personality, big brain, and big hands, was obsessed with learning as much as he could about the function of these microscopic features. His curiosity rubbed off on me, and I began skipping more and more classes in favor of studying the temporal bones with him. To my thinking, I was learning more there than if I had attended all my classes.

In Schuknecht, I felt I'd found a great role model and teacher. I admired his work ethic and devotion to research. We rarely disagreed, unless we talked religion. He was an atheist. I was not. I couldn't shake the religious upbringing of my childhood, and I didn't want to.

"You're a scientist," he'd say. "You can't believe in God."

"I can," I'd say. "And I do."

He'd shake his head at me and chuckle at what he saw as my infantilism.

"I can hold two complex thoughts at once," I'd say.

"All right," he'd concede. "Have it your way."

He grew to like me and appreciate my eagerness to learn, I think. So much so that he offered me a residency with him at Henry Ford after I finished my internship in Oregon.

All these influences, a skipped class here, a willingness to do an extra job there, a connection with one obliging person and then another, helped me crystalize my focus on otology, the study of the anatomy and diseases of the ear. I can't say whether my love of music also inspired my choice, but it's hard to discount that my affinity for music led me, if only intuitively, to studying hearing and trying to help people experience the joys of sound.

I finished my classes with passing grades, and Lynne and I packed up the car. In Portland, Oregon, I dove right in. My sense of comfort and confidence started to develop in my internship. We interns were hands-on, working in the emergency room and in the wards. We had a well-rounded exposure. I also helped and worked part-time with an otolaryngologist in a private practice in Portland, studying the anatomy, diseases, and disorders of the ear, nose, and throat. Most days, he sported a red tie. When I asked him why, he said, "For when I have patients with nosebleeds."

As I had learned earlier, in Blatt's operating room, doctoring can often be a very messy profession. Nothing except "doing it" prepares you for the unexpected spills, spurts, gushes, seeping, and squirts the human body can conjure.

At the hospital, we interns had a lounge with a refrigerator stocked with beer and food—it was a great place to relax, linger, and talk. It was a convenient perk since I worked twenty-four hours on and twenty-four hours off. We also had the privileges of free golf and tennis. During my internship I met a dermatologist with a heavy foreign accent and bushy eyebrows who used hypnosis to relax and treat patients in the emergency room. In the lounge, we'd mess around with hypnosis. He taught me how to do it. I used to practice on Lynne and my friends, and, for a while, I used it to treat certain conditions such as spastic laryngitis, which is basically croup. Sometimes it worked.

Portland was a beautiful, but misty, city. The sun didn't shine frequently. Fine rain showers were common, and they nurtured beautiful rock gardens in front of all the homes, including those in poor neighborhoods. Every kind of weather seemed just a short drive away. We went to the snows of Mount Hood one day and the warmth of the Pacific Ocean at Sunshine Beach the next. I tasted pancakes for the first time in Portland, at a great pancake house. Lynne and I enjoyed the area, even though we knew it was temporary. We made many friends and grew used to the "doctor's life."

Finally, I graduated from my internship. I called my father. "I did it, Pa."

"Now you are a doctor?"

"Yes."

"Now you get a real job?"

I exhaled. "Yes, Pa." I paused. "Well, sort of. I have to do my residency."

He coughed.

The next stop was back to Detroit to start residency at Henry Ford Hospital on July 1, 1958, the launch of my career.

CHAPTER 11

Cat Practice

Detroit is hot and humid in July 1958. In the middle of a hot night, I'm buried in the bowels of an old funeral home with a roomful of purring, meowing, and skeptical farm cats. The fat tabby is Taft. The skinny gray is Jackson. Eisenhower sleeps all day. Ulysses Grant hogs the food. Roosevelt is the calico with rings around his eyes. Jefferson is a scrawny male with a know-it-all attitude. He often defecates in his cage and watches me smugly while I clean up his mess. The cats are my research subjects.

Over weeks and months, I have trained these cats in a rotating cage in this soundproof room to respond to sounds of selected frequencies and intensities (behavioral avoidance conditioning). If they don't run at the given frequency and volume that rotates the cage, I give them a little shock, very mild. They learn quickly. I collect audiograms (hearing tests) from their healthy ears over a period of time.

But I also need audiograms from the cats before and after an experimental lesion operation to make comparisons. So I sedate the cats and cut away the pinnae from their heads. Then they're cats without triangular ears sticking up. They look bald. Their eyes seem bigger, alien-like. In the soundproof room, they seem acutely aware that something has changed. Jefferson licks his paw and wipes where his ear used to be, then licks his paw again. He stares his amber eyes at me. He looks mad. He defecates in his cage again.

In the soundproof room next door, a colleague of mine is taking audiograms from young college women. No removal of the pinnae involved. No cleaning cages.

I pick up Jefferson, pat him on the back, and then set him on the table. I give him an injection of intraperitoneal sodium barbital, a sedative, until he's asleep, and then I expose the middle ear. Using a Cavitron microvibrator, a dental tool I've repurposed for experiments, I stimulate the stapes, the stirrup-shaped bone, creating a lesion. After a few days, Jefferson's ear heals and he settles down. I do a post-stimulation/lesion audiogram to see how the lesion has affected Jefferson's ability to hear.

Afterward comes the real hard part. I again inject Jefferson with a heavy dose of intraperitoneal sodium barbital to anesthetize him. Then, I insert a catheter into his carotid artery, the one that delivers blood to his brain. I depress the plunger. The temporal bone and brain flood with formaldehyde. When Jefferson's lungs and heart stop, I remove the temporal bones of his ear for research.

I feel terrible for days. Though they were "only" discarded farm cats, not pets, I have an emotional attachment to them. But as the observations and measurements and data piles up, I can see how these tests and experiments will benefit humans with hearing loss or deafness, and I thank Jefferson and his companions for their sacrifice in the name of otological advancements to help patients with serious inner ear disorders.

* * * *

I knew almost nothing about research, except for my days recording the durability of airplane tires, but I'd definitely caught the research bug from Schuknecht, who was becoming perhaps the most famous academic otologist in the world in terms of clinical care, education, and especially research. I didn't know it at the time, but Schuknecht was part of a movement that brought about fresh ideas, interest, and ingenuity to the understanding of ear diseases and damage.

The cat experiment I conducted was an adaptation from experiments Schuknecht had performed at the University of Chicago. He would create lesions in the cochlea of felines that were behaviorally conditioned to have audiograms, before and after such lesions. He then transferred to Detroit and continued his research in a rehabilitated funeral home on East Grand Boulevard in Detroit.

I had never done experimentation like this before. Sure, I'd looked at temporal bones and samples under microscopes. But I had never managed an experiment from beginning to end in the way working with the cats forced me to. I focused on learning to independently perform all parts of the experiment, so I thoroughly understood each part. The more I learned, the more comfortable I became. I tried to be as efficient as possible.

Soon it wasn't unusual for me to test six cats in one night. It was exciting to think I was studying something no one else had before. I liked knowing that through my experiments, I was contributing new, and hopefully useful, information to the body of knowledge.

A few months after those experiments, I asked Schuknecht if he could spare a moment so I could quickly explain to him my findings. He was always busy, always working. He barely looked up from his microscope and said, "OK, but make it quick." After I finished describing all aspects and findings of the study, he almost fell off his stool. "You finished all that in a few months?"

"Well," I stumbled. "Yeah."

Schuknecht stuttered. "But that, that … would take years!"

I shrugged. What had he expected? I was a son of the Motor City, the home of Henry Ford, the place and man that perfected efficiency and quality.

"Well," he said. "You know it doesn't mean anything unless it's published." He returned to his microscope. I stood there unsure of what to do. Without looking at me, he said, "Go. Write it down."

So I did. I chronicled every step and finding of my experiment, which resulted in my first publication, "A High-Frequency Microvibrator: Bioacoustical Effects." That paper won the prestigious Kobrak Award, named after the well-known researcher Dr. Heinz Kobrak (one of Schknecht's mentors). Since then, more than 720 publications have followed. To this day, I subscribe to the belief that if you didn't record and publish it, it didn't happen. Or it doesn't matter. Doing research is important. But disseminating it makes the research useful to others.

Getting that first paper accepted for publication lit a fire under me. I wanted to research more and research everything. Schuknecht had a small collection of temporal bones, which include the entire bony structure on the side of your head, with the inner ear. They were from people who had had ear diseases. I studied them to get a better understanding of how those diseases might have manifested, which led me to wonder about their pathogenesis, why they developed in the first place. I did more experiments with animals and conducted deeper research with the existing collection of human temporal bones. This work was very technically challenging.

It occurred to me that even research dissemination could be innovated. So another fellow, Dr. Albert Hohmann from Saint Paul, Minnesota, and I developed a friendship and made a movie with animation demonstrating all the ear operations on the cats that were part of the research. The movie included brain operations that relate to research on hearing. A couple of world-renowned experts helped perform some of the procedures. This film was presented and well received at the field's most important professional organization, the American Otological Society. Later the film was disseminated all over Europe too.

Otology was experiencing a renaissance; it was exciting, and I was there with Schuknecht at the beginning.

The operating microscope became a tool at our disposal. So much easier to see! Drills and other tools were modernized as well. Reconstruction of the eardrum and middle ear were also new advancements. It seemed as if major developments were occurring every other day. I often think about why—what was it about that time period that allowed for such enormous growth in the science?

I like to think one of the reasons was that the medical field was diversifying. What had been a fairly elitist endeavor meant only for the privileged was opening up to people like me, an immigrant's kid, and Schuknecht, the son of a dirt-poor South Dakota farm that had almost blown away in the Dust Bowl.

We brought into the medical sciences a different kind of lens through which we saw the world and through which we solved problems. Our thinking was different from doctors whose fathers had also been doctors or politicians or lawyers. Doctors, in those days, were very much the professional class. That class of society relies upon a sometimes unspoken, rigid hierarchy. Solutions come from the top down.

Schuknecht and I came from a social class that required unhesitating participation and contributions from everyone. So our approach to everything—from inventing tools that didn't exist but that we needed to being researchers as well as practicing doctors—was different.

We were smart, but in a different way than traditional doctors. Schuknecht and I were improvisers and creators. When we didn't have what we needed, we didn't sit around and intellectualize the problem or send a memo on up the line. We made what we needed to get the job done. Based on research from the otopathology lab, we better understood existing and new diseases, which helped us diagnose and treat patients in the clinic and in the operating room.

CHAPTER 12

Call Me Dr. Dad

And now I'm soon to become a father.

I don't really know what to do to prepare, but I know babies cost money. So during my residency I take a part-time job doing home visits and physicals for Lincoln National Life Insurance Company claim owners in the Detroit suburbs.

After my day at the hospital doing rounds and research, I head out to Inkster, Michigan. I pull up to a series of shacks on King Street and take a deep breath before going up to one.

I knock gently on the plywood door.

A cough. "Yeah," someone says.

I say to the closed door, "Good evening, sir. I'm Dr. Paparella with the Lincoln National Life Insurance Company. I'm here to collect your samples and examine you."

"Yeah, it's open."

I tentatively open the door. An old man lies on a dirty couch in a dirty room. He fumbles around for his teeth. When he finds them on the small table, he pops them into his mouth and clanks them around until the fit is right. He stands.

I take his height and guess at his weight. I get his blood pressure. "Sir, I'll need a urine sample."

"Yeah," he says. "Coming right up." He goes behind a curtain that separates one room from another and pees into a milk jug.

"That good?" he asks when he comes back.

"Yes, sir." I take the warm container from him, screw the cover on. "Thank you." And then I hightail it out of there.

Next stop is in a very different suburb, Grosse Ile. I pull in front of a naval officer's mansion.

The door swings open before I can ring the bell. A knockout—dark and buxom—crosses her arms and leans against the doorframe.

"Good evening, ma'am. Is—" I've forgotten his name.

Her mouth curls up and long lashes flutter.

"Is . . . your husband home?"

"Wouldn't you like to know," she says coyly.

"I'm here from the Lincoln National Life Insurance Company, and I had an appointment with him."

"Mmm-hmm," she coos. "Well, I'm not expecting him for some time. Probably not until very, very late. But you can take my vitals and what-have-you."

I swallow the lump of awkwardness that's developed in my throat. "Maybe I'll come back another time, when you're both home."

"Don't be silly. I won't bite."

I hightail it out of there too.

When I get home, Lynne inquires, "How was work today?"

I take out the urine samples to test. "Fine," I say. "Just fine." I worry I might be blushing.

"That's nice," she says.

In a little while, we have enough money to buy a small house on a large corner lot in Taylor, Michigan, for twelve thousand dollars. It was the first time any medical resident in my program bought a house.

I do my very best to be a good homeowner. When gnarly weeds the size of trees take over the edge of the lot, I consult a neighbor in a neighborly way. He advises me that the best way to eliminate these noxious plants is to "get a lot of paper and rags and soak them in kerosene and set them on fire."

Which sounds pretty reasonable to me, so that's what I do.

Thick, black smoke wafts in a terrible ribbon around the neighborhood. Soon other neighbors are screaming at me and asking if I'm an idiot. One of them calls the fire department.

After the flames are extinguished and the smoke clears, I'm slapped with a fine and a lecture.

* * * * *

Pathology is the study of the diagnosis of diseases based on hard evidence, such as changes in body fluids or changes in tissue. Pathogenesis is the study of the origins of the diseases and processes that lead to the pathology. Pathology is the backbone of medicine.

For example, I incorrectly diagnosed the problem of the weeds and thus applied the wrong correction. The problem with weeds is underground, in the roots. So a topical blazing is not going to cure the problem. The roots needed to be killed to eliminate the weeds. Once I figured that out, I had the area bulldozed to dig up the rascals.

Same with disease. We must, to the best of our abilities, understand what's causing a patient's symptoms. We must, to the best of our abilities, understand why the disease manifested. Then we can treat the disease, not just the symptoms.

This might seem obvious, but I can assure you there's a lot of room for improvement in the study of pathology. You might be surprised at how apathetic and lax or simply comfortable doctors and institutions can sometimes be. They inherit an attitude of "This is the way it is" and "This is how we treat it" without ever questioning why or discovering if there's a better way to handle the disease or damage.

Dr. Schuknecht understood this inertia and worked tirelessly toward a full picture of health to come to a correct diagnosis, and thus end unnecessary procedures and medications based on misdiagnosis.

Procedures for hearing loss go back to antiquity. While dissection probably took place before 500 BC, Alcmaeon of Croton, which is in southern Italy, is credited with being the first to conduct a human dissection around 531 BC. He identified the difference between arteries and veins. He speculated that the brain was the impetus for thinking and learning, and he discovered both the optic nerve and the Eustachian tube, which connects the nasopharynx to the middle ear. He also thought that goats breathe through their ears. Despite being incorrect about that, his discovery of the Eustachian tube marks the beginning of otology.

Fifty years later, Empedocles, a Greek philosopher and poet living in Sicily, theorized that all earth's matter could be categorized as earth, wind, fire, or water. He also understood that sounds were vibrations, movements of air, reaching the ear.

Later, in the fourth century BC, Greek philosopher Aristotle read Alcmaeon and decided that he was dead wrong about the way goats breathe, but he was correct about the existence and possibly the function of the Eustachian tube. Aristotle added to the research by suggesting that the cochlea was an internal counterpart to the outer ear. By 690 AD, Paul of Aegina suggested eliminating what must have been a pervasive problem of human earworms using a urine wash. Further advancing the discipline, he also attempted to use venesection, the removal of blood, to cure the "bilious humour" he believed caused deafness. Later he decided congenital deafness was incurable.

Things go on quite ridiculously but interestingly for another seven hundred years or so until Guy de Chauliac, a French surgeon and writer, decided diagnosis and treatment of the ear might be made easier if a guy could see in there. Thus, he invented the ear speculum, the funnel-shaped tool that ENT doctors still use to look inside the ear. By the late 1400s and early 1500s, we have the first attempts at hearing aids, shaped as shells, horns, and cups, and a better understanding of the ear's anatomy.

In the 1680s, a Frenchman named Guichard Joseph Duverney dissected an elephant for the amusement of Louis XIV and also published *A Treatise of the Organ of Hearing, Containing the Structure, the Uses, and the Diseases of All Parts of the Ear*. For this accomplishment, he's considered by many to be the "father of otology."

In the early 1700s, an Italian anatomist named Antonio Maria Valsalva performed autopsies that ultimately contributed to *De aure humana tractatus*, a book that described the anatomy of the ear based on one thousand temporal bone dissections. He is also the name behind the Valsalva maneuver, which is when a person somewhat forcefully attempts to exhale while pinching his nose and closing his mouth, to pop the ear. Today, we use that maneuver for a number of reasons: to test the heart or to clear our ears when ambient pressure changes, but Valsalva thought it would work to remove pus from the middle ear. Soon thereafter, French surgeon Jean-Louis Petit performed the first successful operation for mastoiditis, an infection of the mastoid bone behind the ear.

Centuries pass, with each new generation of doctors learning from the successes and failures of doctors before them. In 1956, Dr. John J. Shea Jr. of Memphis, Tennessee, restored the hearing of a woman with complete hearing loss from otosclerosis, the fixation of the stapes (also called the stirrup) due to a bony growth. He removed the diseased stapes and replaced it with a prosthesis. The woman's hearing was fully restored. This surgery is called stapedectomy.

In July 1958 Dr. Schuknecht performed and innovated his first stapedectomy operation, in which he custom-made the prosthesis using fine steel wire and a wire-bending die with a tiny graft of fat tissue, about two millimeters by three millimeters, donated from the patient's earlobe.

Dr. Schuknecht always had two operating rooms. He believed in learning by doing. So, since I was working in the other operating room and had learned the procedure under his tutelage, at the end of July 1958, I completed my first stapedectomy procedure on a civil engineer. Before the procedure, the patient was deaf, and after the procedure, he was restored to his God-given hearing. Therefore, I was the third person in the world to perform stapedectomy in a patient in the modern era. It was a very exciting moment for the patient, but also for me.

Since Schuknecht and the staff believed that I had "good hands" for surgery, I was concomitantly made a member of the staff as well as a resident. In this way, the hospital could charge independently for my surgical care of patients. I was happy and grateful to receive my salary of three thousand dollars per year.

I asked the civil engineer in whom I first performed stapedectomy what the hospital charged him for his operation. He said it was seven hundred fifty dollars for the surgical portion, about what we collect for stapedectomy today. Can you imagine the financial differential over time?

Later in my residency, in 1961, Dr. Schuknecht directed a very important meeting at Henry Ford Hospital. He asked me to prepare and present a paper on acoustic trauma from surgical instrumentation. I had never given a speech or lectured on anything to anyone before. Hundreds of attendees came to this meeting, including the foremost otologists in the country. Needless to say, I was plenty scared.

I prepared my speech and was driving to the meeting from my home. On the highway, my car began overheating, with white and blue smoke billowing out of the hood. As I eased over to the shoulder, I heard a thumping noise like a hammer striking metal, and the car quit. Gasket blown. I sat there with my speech in my hand, sweating bullets for a while. Finally, I got out of the car and flagged a taxi. I made it to the venue just in time for the beginning of the meeting.

Even though my heart raced and sweat poured, I got the job done. I delivered the speech. It wasn't the best speech anyone's ever heard (though later it was published), nor was my delivery particularly inspiring. But I did it. I learned that if you hope to be taken seriously among decision-makers, you have to get comfortable talking to them.

At the hospital, I was a hybrid, a resident and a staff member at the same time. I performed all aspects of otologic surgery but also did tonsillectomies, sinus procedures, septal deviations, treated head and neck tumors, and so on.

My experience was broad, and my sense of confidence grew.

In 1961, Dr. Schuknecht was appointed professor and chair of the Department of Otolaryngology at the Massachusetts Eye and Ear Infirmary at Harvard Medical School, a most prestigious job. He had come from a farm near Vermillion, South Dakota, and was now to join the elite professors of Harvard. When he was appointed to the position at Harvard, Schuknecht asked me to review his forms, papers, and other application materials, and apply my signature in the appropriate places. I reviewed his grades in college and medical school and was surprised but delighted to see he had a few failing grades. Suddenly I wasn't quite so ashamed of my own lackadaisical study habits. Here was this man, this giant in his field, with poor grades on his transcript. Schuknecht was respected, often feared. If he criticized your paper, for example, at a national meeting, you were humbled. He was the most respected academic otolaryngologist perhaps in the world in the area of research, education, clinical care, and innovations. But it was reassuring to know that he too was imperfect.

Schuknecht wanted me to join him at Harvard on a five-year contract. There were two problems: 1) I didn't know anything about contracts and 2) the first contract I was beholden to was the United States Army's Berry Plan.

The Berry Plan was named for a Harvard graduate and thoracic surgeon named Frank Berry. In 1954, he was promoted to the position of assistant secretary of defense. He developed three pathways toward completion of service. My path meant that the government would not draft me during my medical training. Keep in mind that the United States didn't end the draft until 1973. Even though I wouldn't get drafted for military action, I was still on the hook to serve in the military for at least two obligatory years in my specialty.

Schuknecht, whose parents were German immigrants, was a little dictatorial and felt he could accomplish anything. He took it upon himself to try to control my commitment. He wanted, and I also wanted, to spend my military time with Dr. Ashton Graybiel, a prominent and well-respected researcher with the Navy in Pensacola, Florida. He performed sophisticated vestibular studies in multiple buildings, some of which would actually spin, to study the Coriolis force, the effect of rotation on pilots. I became excited, imagining moving my young family to the warm weather of Florida and the high-tech research opportunities and tools. I began collecting information about where to live, where to get groceries, where to get a beer, where to watch a game. But the army was a formidable entity. The fact that my fate was completely in its hands was inescapable. Even Dr. Schuknecht couldn't take me out of the army and put me in the Navy.

Schuknecht's next plan was for me to work with Dr. Robert Galambos, a world-renowned scientist performing basic auditory studies, including electrophysiology, at Walter Reed Hospital, an army hospital in Washington, DC. Dr. Galambos and I exchanged letters, and he frequently advised me on what I should do to satisfy the "downtown boys," the administrators in the government. So I began to imagine myself in the heart of America's policy-making shenanigans. It wasn't Florida. It was a world-class research facility. I figured out a place to live, but then at the last minute, Dr. Galambos up and quit his job and moved to Hawaii. My opportunity in Washington, DC, had died. Now what?

In my application form, I had emphatically underscored and described how I definitely wanted to stay in the United States. I practically begged not to be sent overseas.

So, of course, I was first assigned to France but ultimately ended up in Nuremberg, Germany. I was determined to make the best of it.

CHAPTER 13

Germany in the Cold War

Christmastime, Germany, 1961.

In this region of the world, two civilizations face off. After World War II, the USSR and the United States rebuilt ravaged parts of Europe and Japan. To the USSR's way of thinking, the United States does nothing more than spread bourgeois capitalism and expand its markets. That's true, to some degree. From the US perspective, the USSR is hell-bent on spreading Marxist socialism to the entire world. Also true, to some degree. Compound that with the fact that neither side communicates with the other very well, and the tension rises. Compound that with the fact that both sides have the capability to wipe out life on the planet with atomic bombs, and you have the makings of an apocalypse.

Nonetheless, Nuremburg is alight with twinkling lights and chirping with Christmas music. Our little apartment is spare, but just enough for my small family. The scent of fried *Weihnachtswurst* (Christmas sausage) and bread hangs in the air. Lynne and I are sharing a bottle of beer after a long day.

"Throw some coal in the unit?" Lynne asks. "Mark's cold, I think." She scoops up our plump little boy, wraps him in a blanket, and peppers him with kisses.

When I was born in 1933, Adolf Hitler rose to power in this country and held his Nazi rallies in this very city. During Mark's infancy, the country of Germany freezes over and the people hold their breath as a cold wall goes up, separating capitalist from communist, neighbor from neighbor, and mother from daughter. It's a terrible thing to watch.

"I will," I say, knowing that as I do, other German residents on the other side of the barrier won't have enough coal for their winter. We watch the construction of the wall on television. Desperate East Germans make dangerous attempts to climb over or sneak through the temporary wall. They jump out of and off the tops of buildings on the east side onto the west side.

Lynne gasps and turns the baby away from the television. "Why won't President Kennedy do anything? Those poor people."

"What can he do?"

"Turn it off," she says.

A man runs into the barbed wire. The sound of gunfire pops just before the screen goes black.

* * * * *

I didn't want to go to Europe. I wanted to stay in the United States to do research, and I wanted to keep my family there. But sometimes duty calls. While I hadn't signed up for the military, a sense of responsibility to my country washed over me. "Ask not what your country can do for you," Kennedy had said, and I took his words to heart. I think I also felt gratitude for the life my country had afforded my father, mother, and our family. The opportunities for freedom, education, and advancement simply weren't possible for us in Italy. America made those things possible.

Before leaving for Europe, I received two weeks of orientation and boot-camp training in the army at San Antonio, Texas. For some reason my paperwork had in-accuracies, and I missed many days of basic training getting it straightened out. When I finally caught up with the rest of my unit, I was far behind. I barely knew which end of a gun was up. My memory of those weeks is hazy. I do recall crawling on my stomach underneath barbed wire while "bullets" flew over my head. I tried very hard to keep my rump clear and be a good soldier. I think I blocked a lot of that experience out of my mind.

The army flew us to Europe in a Military Air Transport Service (MATS) plane that had no windows. I sat backwards. I thought about my father's many trips over the ocean and decided he may have had it slightly better since he had access to fresh air and portholes. In both cases, our families were left behind, to join us later once we were settled.

When the MATS flight landed at Frankfurt, we were immediately taken to the *bahnhof*, the train station.

Bombed-out industrial buildings from World War II were stark reminders of what this region of the world had experienced in the not-so-distant past. We loaded onto the old and rickety train and rattled along to Nuremberg. Upon arrival there, we were sent to a downtown hotel for a couple of weeks. While the city was very beautiful, full of charm, good food, and exceptional beer and wine, I couldn't forget that this was where Hitler held his enormous rallies and shouted maniacally into microphones specifically designed for him, for the unprecedented crowds he attracted. Hitler's words had roared through Nuremberg with emotion. Throngs of people, perhaps some of the people walking around the city with me now, had listened. Had they been alarmed?

Those microphones, Neumann microphones, were a technological breakthrough. Prior to their development, microphones couldn't capture the full range of the human voice. So a man with a high and whiny voice would sound higher and whinier. Hitler needed his tacticians to create an instrument that would lower and deepen his voice while amplifying it. Thus, the development of the Neumann CMV3, or the "Hitler Bottle," as it came to be known. It worked in much the same way the human ear works: when sound enters it, the sound waves move a hair-like diaphragm, which is then converted to an electric audio wave.

If the citizens hadn't been alarmed then, they were now. In fact, the entire country seemed on red alert. Three years before I arrived, Khrushchev demanded that France, Great Britain, and the United States get their troops out of West Berlin by the spring of 1959. Obvious-ly, Eisenhower and the rest of the Western powers de-cided not to comply. In 1960 the Soviet Union shot down an American spy plane. The United States inaugurated a new president, John F. Kennedy, and if Khrushchev thought to intimidate the youngster, he was sorely mis-taken. Khrushchev repeated his prior ultimatum to the new president: You have six months to get out of Berlin. In response, Kennedy activated one hundred fifty thou-sand guardsmen and reservists.

At the end of August 1961, Berliners found themselves standing on either side of a barbed-wire fence. Over the next few months, the barbed wire was encased with ce-ment blocks and concrete. Guard towers hovered over the city. Fortification of another wall, called the inner German border, which crawled from the Baltic Sea to the Czechoslovakian border, began as well. The adjacent land was brightened with floodlights, filled in with sand to detect footprints, and otherwise booby-trapped.

I'm bringing my family into this? If this is the Arma-geddon of my childhood religious teaching, I thought, I may as well do my work until called for the rapture.

Finally, I set my eyes on my home away from home, the 20th Station Hospital in Nuremberg. It was formida-ble, with a tall central building, flanked by two shorter but longer buildings to either side. The entire building was clean and sharp and white. Also, it was enormous, holding more than two thousand beds. As I approached, I noted that the walls were pocked with bullet holes.

Hitler's plan had been for Nuremberg to become the headquarters of his presumed world empire. Accordingly, the 20th Station Hospital was to be the empire's gleaming medical center. Miles and miles of tunnels connected the hospital to the former barracks of SS troops.

I quickly realized I wasn't going to have the luxuries of the Henry Ford Hospital. Modern microscopic ear surgery was new—so new, in fact, I believe I was the first to perform it for the military—and the tools weren't available in the army at that time. So I made do with what they had and quickly got to work inventing my own.

"I need a Bunsen burner," I told a nurse. "And I'll need to order some dental instruments."

She paused before writing it down. "Yes, doctor."

Soon I had that Bunsen flame burning and metal melting, and I was soldering and shaping the dental tools into the hooks, hoes, sharps, points, tweezers, and claws I needed to operate inside the ear canal on the smallest bones of the human body.

I had an old Storz microscope, a product of post-World War II, demilitarized Germany's engineering. In 1945, a young German named Karl Storz opened his first store in Tuttlingen, selling headlamps and binoculars. So many of my early successes and so many of the advancements in the understanding and treating of ear disease in the next decade or so was due to the technological leaps in the years after World War II, when the countries benefitting from the Marshall Plan were able to put money into research and manufacturing rather than tanks, guns, and bullets. The Marshall Plan also opened up the exchange of information, making it possible for doctors previously separated by impenetrable borders to work with and learn from each other. Behind the United Kingdom and France, West Germany received the most postwar economic and rebuilding support under the plan.

With the Storz microscope I was peering deep into the illuminated ear canals of my patients, performing surgeries on officers from Heidelberg, the first of such surgeries in the army in Europe. I got busy. I was allowed to hire a German physician as an assistant, so I spent some time training him the same way Schuknecht had trained me—which is to say fast.

In addition to ear surgery, we did septal operations, sinus procedures, tonsillectomies, and a few more interesting procedures. One night a couple of soldiers went out to the local brewhouse in Garmisch and got competitive over a pretty fräulein. One of the potential suitors bit off the outer ear of the other suitor. Luckily, they had the sense to pick the pinna off the floor and bring it with them to the hospital. I sterilized it, reattached it, and bandaged the young man up and sent him on his way with a stern warning to stop fighting. Well, he did. In the months that followed, though, another of his mates came in with the same injury resulting from the same kind of argument over a German vixen. No word on whether she was the same one or not.

On many occasions career soldiers, such as master sergeants, were referred to me. They'd wave in the general direction of their ears and say they had "some hearing loss." Inevitably, when I measured their hearing audiologically, it was clear they didn't simply have hearing loss. They were totally deaf. Most commonly their deafness was a result of inner-ear damage from being too close to the blasting of 50-caliber machine guns firing from tanks. A gun of that sort produces sound energy of about 150 decibels, an eardrum-rupturing level. The sound waves hit the inner ear like a baseball bat. Humans can hear starting at zero decibels. Ten decibels is breathing. Thirty, whispering. Sixty, normal conversation. At ninety decibels, which is the level of sound created by a running motorcycle, damage to the inner ear is likely after eight hours of exposure.

Most of the officers adamantly denied their deafness, so they could finish their careers to collect their full retirement benefits. I played along.

The 20th Station Hospital was a service hospital, very industrial, with no research opportunities. Since I'd already caught the research bug, I did the best I could with available circumstances, and I mulled topics to explore.

The Germans dread the foehn—fierce winds that barrel down the Alps from Italy. Claims of agitation, migraines, and even psychosis rise when the hot, dry winds blast down the mountain into Germany, casting the region in a slightly blue hue. It was commonly believed among Germans that the foehn affected people's mood and health. Suicide rates increase when it blows in. Hospital visits increase and elective surgeries are cancelled.

I noticed that mucosal cysts in the maxillary sinuses were prevalent among people in Germany. Etiological factors, including the foehn, were considered a possible factor, although I doubted it. So I researched it and wrote a paper in which I also described a method of disrupting these cysts using a frontal-sinus canular device, resulting in a curious publication entitled, "Mucosal Cysts of the Maxillary Sinus: Diagnosis and Management."

I conducted other research on the pathogenesis of otitis media and published other works, including one titled "Unusual Foreign Body of Trachea and Intrinsic Bee Sting of Larynx." The article details the day a soldier came into the hospital with a bit of metal shrapnel lodged in his trachea and how he coughed it out on his own, and then how on another night a solider on late-night guard duty accidentally swallowed a bee from his juice and nearly died from edema. I saved his life with an emergency tracheotomy, which is where you open the windpipe through the neck.

My personal research experience taught me something I rediscovered many times later in life. Research—and, for that matter, any productive activity—is largely intracranial, not intrainstitutional. I had the itch to do research, and so I did, with or without the personnel or technical support of the hospital or the US military.

Surprisingly, they made me an officer in the Officers' Club, which is an honor usually reserved for those with a long army career. Then I was honored by being elected into the Royal Order of the Boar, also generally reserved for career officers. At the initiation, all the officers acted like immature fraternity brothers. For example, during the orientation process, we were obligated to catch a greasy pig in a very muddy area strewn with straw. As we went through the initiation line, the existing members would gently paddle us. A fight ensued when the infamous Colonel John Hall smacked the ass of the head of radiology with unusual vigor. Apparently they didn't like one another. So here we are, all these officers in dress uniforms or semiclad, trying to break up a fight between the colonel of the hospital and the head of radiology. Very undignified.

I met so many strange and wonderful people. I frequently visited Würzberg, Germany, to see Professor Horst L. Wullstein, the pioneer of microscopic surgery and tympanoplasty. While there, I also visited Professor Sigurd Rauch, the pioneer of biochemistry of the inner ear. He would wear a space suit, enter a freezing room, and dissect microscopic particles of the fluids of the inner ear and then conduct chemical analyses on them—yielding some of the most sophisticated and amazing research to date.

We became fast friends. I also visited Düsseldorf and Essen, Germany, where Professor Joachim Heermann was another well-known, innovative ear surgeon. He was an older man who championed exercise. He worked at the Alfried Krupp Krankenhaus, the hospital for the Krupp factory that provided most of the tanks, trucks, and military equipment to Hitler and his Third Reich. The doctor would wear his tall boots and German costume and walk up and down a small mountain in the city. I, panting, tried to keep up with him while we discussed medical matters. His method of surgery was unique. He strapped his patient against the wall and performed surgery in that vertical fashion—to control bleeding, he said. He used palisades of cartilage during tympanoplasty reconstruction. I was able to see the surgery, but not the results in the clinic. Our methods were and are different, but he was a kind and generous host.

I also visited Professor Fritz Zöllner in Freiberg, near the Black Forest. He was the co-innovator of microscopic tympanoplasty surgery, with Wullstein. Eustachian tubal dysfunction is the most important cause of chronic ear infection—such as chronic otitis media, and chronic mastoiditis, which also can lead to serious problems in the ear and temporal bone. Zöllner applied coiled strings into the Eustachian tube to try to improve ventilatory function of the tube, but it didn't work.

Sometimes at universities, I shared my film on the experimental otological surgical procedures on cats. It was a hit. On another occasion, a physician colleague of mine who was of Turkish origin invited me to visit Turkey and his friend, a Mr. Okchuoglu, a civil engineer who lived in a mansion with large stones built by Italian craftsmen overlooking the Bosphorus, a strait that connects the Black Sea with the Sea of Marmara. His job, an important one, was to head a team that dredged the waterway. He was a kind and very religious Muslim who treated me royally. I was honored when he took me with him to a quiet garden where he prayed and contemplated each day.

You'll recall from your geography lessons that on the other side of the Black Sea sits Russia, or the Soviet Union, as it was known then. During that trip, I stood on a bridge over the Bosporus and watched Soviet ship after Soviet ship carrying missiles. Rumor was that the Turkish pilots, who were normally brought on board to navigate the ships through the narrow strait, were bribed with alcohol and caviar to stay away and keep quiet. There was no doubt the ships were going to Cuba.

President Kennedy received his first official photograph of the missiles in Cuba on October 15, 1962, months after I witnessed them in the strait.

Though the Cold War was becoming intense, Lynne and I did our best to ignore it and explore Germany and Europe. I wasn't always working, after all.

We had the opportunity to live in a military billet, but we chose to live in a rental apartment in Fürth, a sister city to Nuremberg, to be among the Germans and better absorb their culture. We made some friends who were German citizens, but also, of course, developed friendships among the various army families. We were overjoyed to welcome our second son, Steven, into the world while there, in 1962. We'd pack up the whole family in a Volkswagen and eat out at simple restaurants in the rural areas and get ourselves tipsy on Oppenheimer Krötenbrunnen, a Mosel wine. We took the boys on trips to the eastern coast of Italy, to Paris, and to Holland. Life was happy out and about, and cozy inside the walls of our apartment.

While Lynne and I generously fed coal into our little heating unit in the winter, we realized our German neighbors kept their apartments pretty chilly. Also, they took cold showers every month of the year. After a shower like that—in a cold house, on a gray and chilly December day, for example—a person's muscles start to tighten up. His face gets stony. He becomes more alert, yes, but also more serious. I began to understand why the Germans made such good beer and drank it so liberally: it warmed them up inside and out.

Even though Lynne and I weren't half as cold as the native Germans, each week we had a case of beer delivered. The bottles had white ceramic flip tops. When you flipped them open, waves of thick clouds wafted up and foamy ones rolled down the sides of the bottles. I've never had a beer as delicious as I did after a long day at the hospital, back at home with Lynne while our little boys toddled around.

The period of time my family and I spent in Germany was a rich and rewarding experience not only culturally but professionally. But, two years in the army was enough for me. While I was encouraged to re-up, I didn't want to do it.

I craved my civilian status. Military protocol was not my cup of tea. All the saluting and "Yes, sir!" and hierarchy and uniforms and protocol felt somewhat superficial to me. Also, I wanted to be closer to my father and siblings, and my mentor, Schuknecht. My father was aging. My siblings too. My nieces and nephews were growing up, and now I had a new son none of them had ever even met. I also dreamt of the research opportunities—the topics, the funding, the labs, the temporal bones—and I wanted desperately to get back to proper investigations. My mind was hungry.

So tired was I of the military, that toward the end of my two-year stint as an obligated volunteer, I began a small demonstration of rebellion. I'd wear my doctor coat rather than my uniform. Maybe it was silly of me, but I was ready to return to my civilian life in America, back to academia and universities, back to practicing with Schuknecht at Harvard, back to where everything made sense, where reason, not tradition, ruled.

Or so I thought at the time.

CHAPTER 14

Temporal Bone Research

Temporal bones, bones, bones. We can learn so much from temporal bones. The three bones of the middle ear, the malleus (the hammer), the incus (the anvil), and the stapes (the stirrup) are so small, all three of them fit on the face of a dime with plenty of space left over. The stirrup is about the size of FDR's ear on the obverse side of the coin.

"Look at these," I say to Schuknecht. I open my briefcase, where I have carefully stored sections of temporal bones that were buried and forgotten in the basement of the hospital at the University of Zurich. Temporal bones encase the middle and inner ears.

"They let you simply walk out with these?" asks Schuknecht, incredulous. He slaps on plastic gloves.

"Yes," I say. "There's more. A lot more."

Schuknecht holds a temporal bone section to his eye. He closes his other eye and stares at the beautiful histopathology.

"If you go, ask for Frau Schmidt," I say. "She'll show you." A week before, I had been in a crypt-like basement even Dracula would have appreciated. Frau Schmidt had shuffled along the dusty, cement, basement floor of the university's *krankenhaus*, favoring one leg and swiping cobwebs and dodging low-hanging light bulbs. She led me to long rows of jars, frozen shut from years of neglect. In each sat temporal bone sections wrapped in onion-skin and preserved in alcohol.

She selected a jar. Wiped it off with her skirt. "*Beachten*," she said, pulling a small hammer from her skirt pocket. She tapped the top of the jar until it cracked and then removed the top to retrieve the sections. Now here I am, back in Massachusetts, sharing my discoveries.

"Look," Schuknecht points with his pinkie at a temporal bone section.

"Yes, it comes from a deaf child." The purpose of my visit to Zurich was to study children's deafness. Then the Germans called it *Taubstumheit*, or deaf mutism, a very inappropriate term since children with hearing loss are as smart as anyone, and can usually speak as well as anyone else.

"Mmm-hmm," he agrees. He turns it from one side to the other. "How old?"

"The temporal bone?" I shrug. "Probably late 1800s or early 1900s. Iodine deficiencies were common in the Alps region. The deficiency was related to Pendred syndrome."

He sets the section down and picks up another, stares at it as a coin collector might gaze upon a rarity. Then he stares down at me. He's tall; I'm not so tall. I swallow the lump in my throat.

He smiles at me. "Very good," he says.

This was the beginning of my personal collection of human temporal bones that later developed into one of the largest in the world. Schuknecht was so impressed he later visited the University of Zurich and its krankenhaus more than once and obtained unstained sections that he added to his collection of temporal bones at Harvard. To date, the active collections at Harvard and the University of Minnesota are the two largest in the world, attracting visiting doctors and scientists throughout the globe because they are so rare.

* * * * *

May I tug your ear about a rather macabre subject? Death. Or rather, how to be a good citizen of humanity after death.

Otopathology—clinical research that provides critical information that helps in diagnosis and treatment of many ear diseases that are disabling and very common in our and other societies—is nearly totally dependent on the procurement of temporal bones. Doctors and researchers can learn many things from animal studies and animal bones; but, to be blunt, we especially need human temporal bones.

I understand this makes you squeamish, especially if you consider the unholy history of getting cadavers for study. In the Middle Ages, the worst capital punishment one could receive was to have his body not only killed but then publicly dissected. The indignity was enormous. It was not only a punishment for the criminal, but was also a way to continue punishing the family of the deceased. Later, in Europe and the United States, bodies from prisons or asylums were "donated" for anatomical studies, with or without the blessing of the deceased or his family. In other areas, grave robbing was common, particularly from the cemeteries of the poor or minority parts of town. In New York City in the late 1700s, a horde of angry citizens attacked the New York Hospital and beat medical students and doctors after an unfortunate event. A little boy had passed near the window of a medical student performing an autopsy. The medical student, stupidly, raised the hand of the cadaver to wave it at the boy, who ran home to tell his father. Father and son went to the cemetery to visit the grave of their recently departed wife and mother, only to find it empty. The father connected the dots and rallied a mob.

Here in Minnesota, where I live and work now, on December 26, 1862, after a series of bloody battles between German settlers and Dakota warriors, thirty-eight Dakota men were hung in Mankato. They were buried in a mass grave in the sandy shores of the Minnesota River. By morning, all of the bodies had been excavated at the direction of several doctors, including William Mayo, the father of the brothers who founded the famous Mayo Clinic in Rochester, Minnesota. The event and its aftermath remain a painful memory for many Native American people.

States started to legislate the attainment of cadavers. Doctors began to try and convince living people to donate their bodies to science for the greater good. In 1912 two hundred doctors from New York publicly announced that they were donating their bodies for dissection to normalize the practice. Still, the public didn't warm to the idea of voluntarily giving up their body parts for research. Interestingly, it was the rising cost of funeral arrangements that made people reconsider the option. Especially during hard economic times, people decided they didn't want to be a financial burden on their families after death.

These days, one can identify on a driver's license whether or not the individual is an organ donor (though, sadly, not for human temporal bones). But, still, we need to go further in helping people understand the importance of this last gift. I think doctors can do a lot to help the cause by approaching the matter with respect and gratitude. Above all, we must help the public understand that we treat every donor with dignity, and that each donor's sacrifice is a gift to human health.

Recently, questions of the ethical use of research materials and even body samples from Josef Mengele's victims arose in Munich. Jars of brains and body parts from Jewish concentration camp victims were discovered at a German institute with a long history of research in neuropathology. Unfortunate instances like this one set us back in our efforts to persuade individuals to become donors.

But I can assure you that I, my colleagues, and every student I've trained approach the procurement, dissection, and study of the human body with the utmost respect. We understand that this gift comes from a person and a family who feel a social responsibility toward bettering human health.

Pathology is the backbone of medicine. Whether the study material is tissue or a temporal bone from an autopsy, a frozen section, or material derived from the operating room, the research reveals the definitive diagnosis of disease, be it cancer or an infection or an inherited abnormality or something else. Pathology makes it possible to be more certain about the causes of health problems and appropriate treatments. Pathology seeks to eliminate guesswork.

The human temporal bone is the most difficult part of the body to study pathologically. The cellular contents of the ear, both in the middle ear and especially the inner ear (including the cochlea and the vestibular labyrinth), are some of the most delicate in the body, and they're surrounded by one of the hardest unique bones, the shell of the inner ear. Thus, the challenge is to first acquire the temporal bone, and then to process, section, and study it.

Temporal-bone studies in my own lab have improved the treatment of otitis media, chronic otitis media, and all the various aspects of ear infections that are perhaps the most common diseases affecting people all over the world. In developing countries, people still die from these diseases because they lead to meningitis, brain abscess, and facial paralysis. Our studies have also advanced the discovery of new diseases, which aids the overall goal of treating patients correctly. Advances in research help us avoid treating patients for something they don't have, based on symptoms that manifest in many diseases.

Silent otitis media and middle ear/inner ear interactions are two diseases that we first saw, described, and named in our lab. Our first of many research studies demonstrated how the various types of ear infection can progress along a continuum from childhood otitis media—characterized by different types of fluid behind the eardrum—to much more serious chronic otitis media with chronic mastoiditis and associated tissue (tumor-like) pathology, which can be serious. All of the pathology described in the existing medical literature required the presence of a perforation of the eardrum and drainage (otorrhea). Our research clearly demonstrated that you can have serious pathology behind an intact eardrum and no drainage. Thus, we were able to diagnose and treat many patients who hitherto were not diagnosed to have a significant ear disease.

Animal and human temporal-bone studies also clearly indicated for the first time that infection and other diseases in the middle ear can spread through the round window membrane to cause nerve (sensorineural) deafness as well as balance or dizziness problems, again helping many patients with these often serious problems that weren't identifiable before these studies. Our lab has also helped us to diagnose and treat more common diseases such as Ménière's disease, which causes deafness, vertigo, pressure, and tinnitus that can destroy a person's life.

The scientific jargon gets a little heavy, I know. So, let's step back and make it more personal.

Imagine you're a thirty-year-old road construction worker. Let's say you're driving a belly dump. Let's say your truck carries twenty tons of sand. Now imagine that as you're driving a load of sand to be dumped precisely between a concrete wall and a precipitous drop-off, without warning, you feel as though you're spinning. The spinning is akin to the sensation you might experience after a long night of drinking and have finally collapsed in bed. Except, you haven't had a drink since last weekend. But you're spinning, wildly.

Other trucks, ready to unload, are lined up behind you. You stop the truck, close your eyes, and wait it out. Maybe if you're lucky, the vertigo passes in only a few minutes.

What if after this episode passes, after you successfully dump the sand between the two dangerous barriers, you start driving your eighteen-wheeler and suddenly, again without warning, you think you hear horns, whistles, and sirens. You might begin the tedious process of braking and slowing your truck down again. You check your mirrors, but there's no foreman, no police officer, no reversing truck. Nothing that would have been the source of the noise. Over the next couple of weeks, these episodes increase. And now you're also experiencing intermittent deafness and a sense that your head is full and feels like it might explode. The job must be done on time. There are no replacement workers. You need the paycheck, and you've already used up your sick pay and vacation time so you could be home when your baby was born. What do you do?

More than six hundred thousand people have Ménière's disease in the United States alone. Its effect on daily life is tremendous. We know this disease is rooted in the inner ear and that fluid buildup causes the symptoms, and we're getting ever closer to identifying its causes by studying its pathology and pathogenesis. While it can be triggered by trauma, it is usually not. Our research indicates it to be largely genetic in most, if not all, cases, characterized by endolymphatic hydrops (fluid buildup in the inner ear).

Previously the typical audiogram for a patient with Ménière's disease was a low-tone or flat audiometric pattern. We reported how many patients, at least half, have a peak audiometric configuration at two thousand cps, which can not only be helpful diagnostically but can also be a prognosticator of surgical outcome. We also described the histopathology of how Ménière's disease can be associated either causally or coincidentally with other diseases, such as chronic otitis media, trauma, or otosclerosis. Anatomical studies of human temporal bones have led to some important information that contributed to an operation I developed named endolymphatic sac enhancement (ESE), which has helped thousands of patients with incapacitating Ménière's disease.

But we still can't cure it. And we want to. We need human temporal bones to do so.

While individuals are relatively open to donating their kidneys, their eyes, various parts of their bodies to service and research, they don't often think about the temporal bones. Some worry it is a disfiguring process.

It's not. The skullcap is removed and the temporal bones are detached with no disfigurement to the body. This can occur in either the hospital or the funeral home. It is more important than ever that individuals donate their temporal bones, especially if they have ear diseases. That way, we can study the disease in the temporal bone and then, through correlative studies, prospectively and carefully, we can apply that information to living human beings. In my opinion, that has been the most helpful method of research to diagnose and treat the many hundreds of diseases that occur in otology and neurotology. This science is in desperate need of a reawakening if we want to continue revolutionary improvements to some of the most common human health challenges that manifest from those tiny auditory places inside your head. Sadly, only three active temporal bone research laboratories currently exist in the world—in Boston, Minneapolis, and Los Angeles. We need more.

CHAPTER 15

To Boston with Schuknecht

After two years in the army, the next stop was Boston, happily. While I'd been in Germany, Dr. Schuknecht again invited me to join him at Harvard. This time, that move was possible. I just had to take the American Board of Otolaryngology examination first. The exam takes a couple of days and is critical for specialists to achieve board certification, which is necessary for hospital privileges and status. It's also the scariest test a specialist takes, requiring months and years of study. A significant percentage of specialists, usually 20 percent or more, don't pass.

Recall, if you will, my less-than-stellar study habits. I hadn't studied for the "months and years" that most of my cohorts had. I didn't burn the midnight oil memorizing the various symptoms of the rarest ear diseases. Lynne didn't have to lift my drooling face off thousand-page textbooks and gently coax me to bed while my brain swam with dreams of the inner ear. I couldn't be found at the library at the crack of dawn, waiting for it to open so I could go in and pore over dusty medical journals. No, I'd never been and was never going to be that kind of learner. What I did was continue seeing patients. I listened to them. I examined them. I helped them. And I studied temporal bone histopathology.

In the days before the exam, I flipped through the most popular otolaryngology textbook of the time, *Diseases of the Nose, Throat and Ear*, edited by Dr. Chevalier Jackson and his son Dr. Chevalier L. Jackson, pioneers of bronchoesophagology.

When preparing to take the boards, I shared a hotel room at the Palmer House in Chicago with two friends and colleagues, Dr. Roy Hayden and Dr. Werner Chasin. Roy Hayden, from Minnesota, was an A+ medical student who was my junior resident at Henry Ford Hospital, and for some strange reason he wasn't accepted for residency at the University of Minnesota. He once recorded a B on an examination and was alleged to have almost jumped off the Washington Avenue Bridge into the Mississippi River because of his disappointment. He was wound tight. Perhaps unsurprisingly, he passed the boards and opened a private practice in Detroit, but he died of a heart attack at an all-too-early age. When I heard about this, I was head of otolaryngology at Minnesota; I went into the bathroom, cried, and kicked the wall.

Later Werner Chasin and I shared an office at the Massachusetts Eye and Ear Infirmary. Werner was a super-intellect—he not only knew everything about otolaryngology, he would attend conferences in internal medicine and other specialties and learn about those fields as well. Incidentally, the office we shared looked over the roof of the jail next to the infirmary. One day, while staring out the window, he became giddy.

"Paparella!"

I ignored him.

"Paparella!" He waved his arms wildly. "Get over here."

I looked up from my papers. "I'm busy. What do you want?"

"*Get over here.*" He pointed out the window. "Look at this!"

I sighed and stood. When I got to the window, I looked to where he was pointing.

Like a strand of ants, prisoners in blue uniforms were creeping along the jail's roof. They were crouched over and swift.

"What the—"

"There's nowhere for them to go," Werner said. "Those guys are toast."

I didn't know these men from Adam, but somewhere deep inside, I almost wanted them to succeed, to escape, to taste a bit of freedom. Instead, lights and sirens began wailing and flashing. Armed police officers in riot gear poured out of the prison with guns aimed at the escapees, who dropped to their knees and put their hands in the air.

"Ah, that's too bad," said Werner. "I almost wanted them to get away with it."

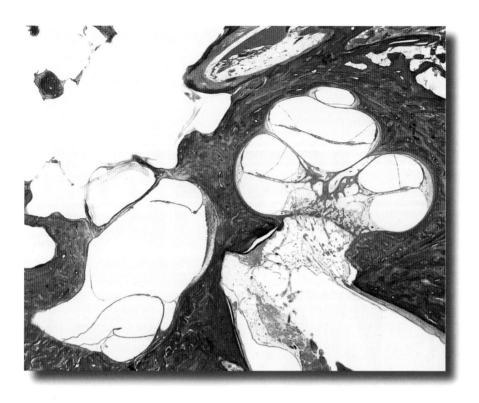

This shows the middle section of a human temporal bone. The detailed cells are carefully studied for research, which benefits patients with ear diseases like deafness and vertigo. The pink color represents the hardest bone in the human body. The white spaces represent (top left): the middle ear, which transmits sound to the inner ear; (top right): the cochlea, with its turns, for hearing; (left white space): vestibular labyrinth, for balance; and (right lower space): the internal auditory canal, where hearing and balance nerves connect the brain to the inner ear.

My maternal grandfather, the head of the eight-track train station in Castel di Sangro.

My mother and father's wedding photo in Castel di Sangro, in the province of Abruzzi, in Italy.

My baby picture.

My father's grocery and dry goods store in Berwick, Pennsylvania.

Practicing my trumpet on the back porch at age nine.

My siblings in a photo taken during World War II.
Josephine, the eldest, is on the left, Elsie is on the right,
and Anthony (Tony) is kneeling with me.

My mother and
father at my
sister's wedding.

In my army uniform
with my dad in the
backyard.

My first wife, Lynne.

My great sons, Mark (left) and Steven (right).

My daughter Lisa with her mother Rebecca.

John Anderson, my tennis partner for years, on the left, and Nick Bollettieri in the middle. John and I would sometimes skip a research meeting to attend the Bollettieri tennis camp in Bradenton, Florida.

As a tennis fan, I was happy to meet Chris Evert at her charitable foundation tennis event.

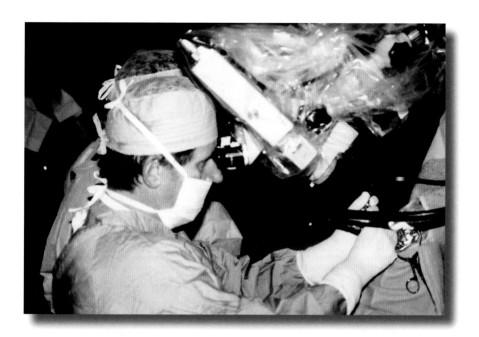

Here I perform microscopic ear surgery, most often for intractable Ménière's disease and chronic otitis media.

Harold F. Schuknecht, MD, my mentor, colleague, and friend, with me at a private meeting held by Dr. John Shea in Memphis, Tennessee, to commemorate the fortieth anniversary of stapedectomy.

Studying human temporal bone sections with the
fellows in the research laboratory.

My greatest satisfaction comes from educating doctors. So
many of them are not just colleagues but friends. Left: Luiz
Carlos Alves de Sousa, MD, medical director, Paparella Clinic
(Ribeinao Preto-Sao Paulo, Brazil), and former professor and
dean of the medical school at Unaerp University (Brazil). Right:
Sady Selaimen Da Costa, chairman and clinical professor,
Department of Otolaryngology, School of Medicine, Federal
University of Rio Grande Do Sul (Brazil).

At the international meeting on Ménière's disease in Rome, where I was an honored guest speaker for a third time. My bonus was to spend personal time with Pope Francis.

Memories — 1996
"Saint" Mother Theresa
Calcutta, India

Treva and I had a personal forty-five minute visit with Mother Teresa, a remarkable and wonderful saint. She passed into heaven six months later.

Treva, my beautiful wife, inside and out, with me at a
Starkey gala produced and directed by Bill and Tani Austin
to raise funds for charity and missionary work.

Meeting Mickey Rooney and Elton John at
another Starkey gala with Treva.

"Yeah. Me too, I guess."

Whenever I talked to Dad on the phone, he gave me updates on my siblings, of course, but often he'd talk about the other kids from the neighborhood and what had become of them. Most worked in factories. Rarely, one or two went to jail. I wondered sometimes why my old friends ended up in these places, but not me. What had gone differently in my life? We hadn't had more money than those families. We hadn't had a better place to live.

Hayden and Chasin continued to prepare for the exam. All day long and late into the night, they'd pepper each other with questions about rare syndromes and details I'd never heard of. And they knew all the answers.

Having reviewed only one textbook, Jackson and Jackson, taking the board examination, which is usually scary, became super scary.

On the day of the exam, I remained calm and answered all the questions—too quickly, I thought. I left the exam unsure. If you'd told me I got every single answer right, I would've believed you. If you'd told me I got nearly all of them wrong, I'd have also believed that.

I passed.

So off to the Massachusetts Eye and Ear Infirmary I went to join Schuknecht.

The cold water, cold apartments, and Cold War of Nuremburg had nothing on the atmosphere I walked into.

Before I arrived, I found out, a doctor named George Reed, a head and neck cancer surgeon, was expected to inherit the coveted title "Professor and Chairman of the Department of Otolaryngology Head and Neck Surgery."

Reed had a Harvard pedigree, had been at the Eye and Ear Infirmary for years, and fully expected to be granted the position.

Instead, Hal Schuknecht, originally from a wind-blown, Dust Bowl farm in South Dakota before becoming a professor and chairman at Harvard in 1961, got tapped to run this prestigious department. As I said, Schuknecht and I had a lot in common. We were common people, from common fathers, from the common fields and factories of the Midwest. We drank beer. We spoke plainly and sparingly. We worked hard. We researched by inspecting and dissecting temporal bones. We learned by doing.

Compared to some of the shiny-shoed, slick-haired, careful articulators at Harvard, we were not "Bostonians."

Schuknecht wasted no time asserting his will without the pleasantries of typical highbrow settings. His academic abilities and potential were unquestionable, but his personality was sort of "my way or the highway." George Reed complicated the politics by developing a private practice in a facility contiguous to the Eye and Ear Infirmary. The surgeons who rotated and ran the clinical services at the hospital were mixed, some for and some against Schuknecht. Nevertheless Schuknecht barreled ahead, intent on instilling and enhancing a strong academic program at Harvard, especially in research, but also in clinical services and education.

Of course, I supported Schuknecht 100 percent, but I proceeded with the respect a son gives his father. I watched and listened to him carefully. But I also thought about ways I'd do it differently if I ever had the chance.

So when Schuknecht returned from an international meeting and decided it would be best to decompress the facial nerve in all patients with Bell's palsy to hasten the recovery of facial function, I followed his instructions even though I disagreed. I'd observed that the majority of patients who develop the facial paralysis of Bell's palsy recovered spontaneously with the assistance of steroids and time. But I knew better than to contradict him directly. So I hesitatingly assisted residents in these decompressions a number of times. Rather quickly, he adopted the more standard approach.

The chilly atmosphere persisted, but so did the work of the clinic.

We had a patient who came in time and time again with severe external otitis, a chronic infection of the ear canal. The canal was completely blocked with swollen tissue and drainage.

The poor man couldn't hear. He was in constant, terrible pain. Antibiotics, medications, many dozens of ear wicks and the like were all attempted, but the infection persisted. I decided to try something, a canalplasty in which I removed all the problem tissue and enlarged the bony canal, its opening. Then I'd do a thin skin graft from his arm to line the canal walls.

As I operated on the man, I found a small tumor buried underneath the soft tissue. The chronic swelling and drainage had kept it hidden. I removed it and completed the canalplasty as planned. The patient had an excellent result. I wrote a few papers on this technique and the indications for intractable external otitis. It was published, making it possible for other patients to benefit from the procedure.

Schuknecht lost some support at Harvard when he fired a beloved doctor, Dr. Werner Mueller, who was chief of pathology. The doctor was a board examiner and well respected nationally as an educator in pathology, but he wasn't a basic researcher. Therefore, he was fired and replaced with a histochemist. In the aftermath, the schism widened at the clinic. Even though labs were right next to each other, nobody was sharing information. They didn't even communicate. Opportunities for collaboration were missing.

Right then and there I decided if I had to deal with similar problems later in my career, I would do the opposite and find whatever good I could in individuals and try to nourish and support it—sometimes, as I found out in the future, to my own detriment. It is one thing to be a thorough researcher, a great doctor, and a good teacher. Being a leader is an enormous challenge that requires constant adaptability.

Nevertheless, we were in the epicenter of otological discoveries and progress and much of it revolved around Schuknecht. This era encompassed some of the fastest-developing and most exciting advancements in research on ear disease and hearing loss. Schuknecht was a scientific-solutions thinker. If he saw a problem, he slapped a solution on it. But scientific and technical solutions don't always address the wider adaptive change in thinking required among the human beings involved in making the technical solutions more widely used and more successful. Despite some people's resistance to Schuknecht's leadership style and methods, under his tutelage the department grew and flourished.

I kept my head down and focused on learning as much as possible and honing my own skills as a researcher and surgeon. In terms of scholarship, I was in good company. Besides the ongoing mentorship of Schuknecht, who was on his way to resurrecting the field of research otology with his focus on pathology, I was lucky to be locker neighbors with Dr. Varaztad Kazanjian.

Kazanjian graduated from the Harvard School of Dentistry in 1905. He was an Armenian who'd escaped the atrocities against his people by the Ottoman Empire. In the United States, he took a job in a wire factory to pay his way through school and then opened his own dental practice. When World War I broke out, Kazanjian volunteered his services to help the soldiers wounded in battle. Near some of the fiercest battles in France, he set up a rudimentary hospital in a tent to treat the battered men. He quickly realized he was going to have to be creative, clever, and a little bold because so many of the young men needed far more than ordinary dentistry. They needed reconstruction of their jaws, eye sockets, noses, lips, and cheeks. Dr. Kazanjian began practicing and pioneered what we now call plastic and reconstructive surgery. When I considered his trajectory, I couldn't help but think about how great this country was: a place where a refugee from a massacre could become an internationally revered plastic surgeon pioneer.

Despite the office politics, my life was good in Boston. Lynne and the boys and I rented a modest home in Newton Corner. I drove to work each day along the Charles

River to 243 Charles Street, address of the Massachusetts Eye and Ear Infirmary. Everything you've ever heard about Boston streets, traffic, and drivers is true. I'm a defensive driver, yet other drivers would shout and yell at me. Everybody was always cutting in front of me, swearing at me, and using the middle finger readily, though I hadn't done anything wrong.

Toward the end of 1963, Dr. William Saunders, chair of otolaryngology at Ohio State University in Columbus, offered me a job. He wanted me to be his first clinical associate and the first otologist in the department. He wanted help starting clinical ear research in that department.

On November 22, 1963, President Kennedy was shot and killed in Dallas, Texas. The whole country was appalled, but the people of Boston and Harvard, in particular, where the Kennedy family had lived and learned, were stupefied. For a moment, even though we didn't yet understand who had killed him or why—or what it meant in the grand scheme of world events—it felt as though violence was much too close to my family. Lynne sat on the couch with Mark, who was three, and Steve, only one and a half, on her lap and watched the news come in.

"I'm going to go to Ohio," I told her. "To see about that job."

"Yes," she nodded. "It's in the middle of nowhere. Yes. Let's go there." She buried her teary eyes into the top of Steve's baby hair. On the screen, over and over again, Jackie Kennedy picked pieces of her husband's brain off the back of the car.

CHAPTER 16

Difficult Days, Difficult Decisions

I'm high over the middle of America. I drum my fingers on my knees and wait for the plane to glide through the low clouds and descend in Boston. I'm overwhelmed with a sense of foreboding.

Hours ago, I accepted the position at Ohio State University as assistant professor and director of the otopathology lab, which I was to launch and develop. While still reeling from the significance of that decision, I took a phone call from Lynne's sister, who had come to help her with the boys while I was in Columbus.

Her voice was shaking. "Can you come home?"

"Now? I just got—"

I could hear that her breathing was shallow, as though she'd been crying.

"Wait. What's wrong?"

"It's Lynne," she said. "There's something . . ."

"Judy. What's happened to Lynne? Where are the boys?"

"The boys are fine. They're with me."

"What's wrong with Lynne?"

"It's her head." She paused. "She said she had a headache and then—"

"Is she all right?"

A long pause.

"Judy?"

"I don't know. She's not well. Can you come back?"

"I'll be there as soon as I can."

I enter Massachusetts General Hospital not as a doctor, but as the husband of a woman who has suffered a massive cranial bleed.

Dr. Sweet, Lynne's neurosurgeon, tells me a blood vessel in her brain developed a sac that ballooned and then exploded, causing hemorrhaging at the base of her brain.

"She's lucky to be alive," he says.

When I look down at my comatose wife, I see the woman I love and the doting mother of my boys. I see the woman who has followed me over the ocean and back again and the woman who has supported my every career move. Will she still be in there, I wonder. I can't help it, but I also think of my mother. I think about how her brain failed her. How she didn't live long enough to see her grandsons.

After Dr. Sweet leaves, I sit with Lynne and hold her hand. After a while, a long shadow appears in the doorway. Then a gentle knock. It's Schuknecht.

I stand up. He embraces me.

"They called me as she was going into surgery," he says. "I saw the whole thing. I'm sure you know . . . it doesn't look good. He packed the aneurysm with gauze and some Japanese glue material." He shook his head.

We both stare at her. We listen to the breathing machines.

"I took the job in Columbus," I say.

After a few seconds, he reaches up and slaps my shoulder. "You'll be great there." His huge hand holds on to my shoulder. "Whatever you need. I'm here for you. Ann and I are both here for you."

I nod because my mouth is too dry to talk anymore.

For days, I walked around Boston Commons in a stupor. Lynne had a very difficult time in the hospital, was neurologically crippled and in a coma, and after she did come to, was aphasic, unable to talk. I had to make all major decisions about her and about our family on my own. The doctors warned me that her neurological damage would more than likely be significant and her recovery slow. I remember thinking that aside from being there for her and my boys, the most important thing I had to do was keep a steady income coming in to pay for her and the boys' care. As soon as she was released from the hospital, we would go to Ohio.

We bought a modest home in Worthington, a suburb of Columbus, and I would drive back and forth to and from work along the Olentangy River Road just as I had along the Charles River in Boston. July 1964 was the beginning of a very trying period, personally and professionally.

Over weeks and then months, Lynne's communication slightly improved, but she was disabled. I was trying to start a career at Ohio State University and keep our family above water. The boys were small and quite a lot of work. Mark was now four, curious about everything and old enough to understand that Mom wasn't quite right. Her condition was very difficult for him. "Mom," he'd say. "Mom, watch me." She'd stare and search for words she couldn't make. "Mom?" Those were hard days. Steve was two, a crackle of energy and bad ideas. He had no concern for his own safety. Should he climb on top of the table? Yes. Should he climb on top of the chest of drawers? Yes. Should he stand on top of the kitchen cupboards? Yes. Should he stand precariously at the lip of the top step and laugh maniacally while I race to grab him before he tumbles down? Yes.

While I had enormous energy at work, he wore me out. He wore all of us out.

Luckily, Lynne's parents helped a lot and then we hired Margaret, a full-time helper to take care of the house, the children, and especially Lynne, which allowed me to work and pay the bills. Her clinical care and support was constant, and we also consulted the chair of neurosurgery at the university. She received excellent care, but progress was very, very slow. The Lynne I'd married seemed lost to me.

At night, after the kids would go to bed, I'd try to connect with her, but she seemed angry all the time, so the words that did come to her often made me want to leave in the middle of the night and go back to the office. Sometimes she said odd things, like when she was sure she'd seen Jesus in the backyard. I didn't know what to do. I didn't know how to help her.

Over time, Lynne improved very slowly, mostly in gaining some use of her arms and legs, but she began to manifest more symptoms of brain damage, including moments of rage and delusional periods. Her aphasia improved slowly. Mark and Steve managed to grow up nicely in spite of this trauma, and Mark started kindergarten and then entered first grade. Mark was an ambitious young child, and at the age of five he discovered a large front-end loader on a lot near our home, climbed up on the high seat, turned the engine on, and was driving the vehicle. Fortunately, the police stopped him before he knocked down a house. Another time, Mark took Kapper, the pet dog, out for a walk and to the swing set. Mark was playing on a swing. A high school kid with a German shepherd came by and commanded his dog to attack Mark, who was only a small boy. Kapper, though much smaller than the German shepherd, attacked and bit the larger dog in a delicate location, and the big dog ran away yelping, perhaps saving Mark's life. We lavished attention upon our "good dog" and "courageous protector."

* * * * *

I guess I threw myself into my work at Ohio State. Maybe to take my mind off the difficulties at home. I hired new people. I got the lab up and running. I set up two rooms for surgery, just the way Schuknecht had taught me, so I could teach my own residents and provide optimal care to patients. I lectured medical students and residents. We researched and experimented to innovate several certain methods of diagnosis and surgical care.

My office at Ohio State was in an old building with a lovely name, Starling Loving Hall, which also had six strange gargoyles: a bunny, a cow, a stork, a cat, a monkey, and a horse. While working in the Tudor-style building, I never wondered who Starling Loving was, but I admired the name. The building's original uses included a research lab, a maternity ward, and a morgue. Rumor was that the building was haunted with dark shadows in the halls, whispering specters, screaming phantoms of mothers who died in childbirth, and the ghosts of animals used in experiments.

I brought all my temporal bone sections with me from Harvard and moved them into the building. They would become the foundation of the research laboratory for pathology that I was to create here. Since my office and laboratory were right next to the Pathology Department, I was subject to frequent interruptions by the head of that department, an Italian-American like me. He liked me because of my Italian last name. I liked him too, and I admired him as a scientist—but, boy, was he a loudmouth. I couldn't believe how the words poured from his mouth.

Frankly, I just didn't feel like conversation much in those days. What was I going to say? *My wife is very sick. My boys are very small. I'm new here. I'm trying to find my place. I need to make money. I just bought a house. I have a lot of responsibilities.* No. I wasn't going to say those things. I kept my nose to the grindstone and worked. I'd smile and nod silently at colleagues and then stare down at the sections until they went away. When that was impossible, I'd sometimes sneak away to the football stadium to watch Coach Woody Hayes and his Buckeyes.

At home, Kapper the dog was a beloved part of the family. At work, though, animals were for learning; we had a lab devoted to animal experimentation. While I know this makes some people uncomfortable, as I discovered through my original experiments on cats, we can learn so much about disease pathology and treatment from them. Though Schuknecht's research, interests, and activities were in the inner ear, he didn't believe the most common diseases of the middle ear—such as otitis media or chronic otitis media, which affect children and adults frequently—were a significant area for research. I did.

Otitis media is a common disease in the United States and in all countries of the world. It can cause deafness, complications in the inner ear such as vertigo, and although rare in America but common in second and third-world countries, otitis media can cause intracranial complications and even death. I thought it should be a fertile field of research and important in our field. Alongside research using human temporal bones to correlate with otological clinical problems in patients, we were also active with animal research to gain insight regarding human disease.

The animal experiments—on cats, monkeys, and guinea pigs—mostly took place in a separate research building directed by Dr. Stilton. Thus, in a mode of dark doctor humor, we referred to the building as the "Stilton Hilton." It was, as I recall, extremely expensive to use that facility, and we had to be frugal. Often more than one kind of experiment would be conducted on one animal. One of our residents performed radical sinus surgery in the frontal and ethmoid sinuses in pigs. He would then surgically remove the entire sinus and apply a skin graft against the exposed brain in the pig. To be economical, other research residents used these pigs for burn experiments. At the end of the experiments, the conclusions were celebrated with a pig roast at the edge of town. No part of the pig went to waste.

Otopathology study and experiment and the subsequent publications that related their findings have contributed to the correct diagnosis and treatment of millions of people with many hundreds of different kinds of ear diseases and syndromes. The National Institutes of Health (NIH) estimates that ninety million Americans suffer dizziness or vertigo, usually emanating from issues in the inner ear (labyrinth); forty million Americans suffer from tinnitus, unwanted buzzing or ringing noises, which has led certain patients to suicide; and forty million Americans have significant hearing losses or deafness that can come from multiple causes—genetic, traumatic, illness, aging, or a combination of factors. Research is key to helping those people live their lives as fully and pain-free as possible.

Recalling one of my first publications on enzymes in serous otitis media from research in Nuremberg, I continued to emphasize studies of otitis media, both basic and applied. The only other otologist interested in otitis media at that time that I was aware of was Dr. Ben Senturia, a friend and colleague in Saint Louis, Missouri. In 1963, I applied for my first independent grant, "Pathogenesis of Serous Otitis Media," and it was funded. As far as I can tell, this was the first NIH grant to study otitis media.

Prior to 1964, I had assisted, when I could, Schuknecht's international research fellows. Now I began my independent quest to teach international fellows. My first independent fellow was Dr. David J. Lim, who ultimately became perhaps the most-respected research leader worldwide. He had his MD and ENT training in Korea. David stumbled into Columbus in 1964. He wanted to study audiology, and he was chasing a pretty young girl, Yung Sook, who eventually became his wife. I was successful in convincing him that otopathology and research in otitis media was important.

At that time, I always encouraged and supported research by the residents as well. One of my other early fellows was Dr. Kawabata, who did pioneering work on electron microscopy of the round window and the middle ear cleft. Another was Dr. Hoshino, who was productive in research on otitis media. They both became professors and departments chairs, and leaders in Japan.

After his initial exposure to otopathology, I called Dr. Robert S. Kimura, a dear friend and expert in electron microscopy at Harvard, to help train David Lim. This training and his experience with Schuknecht was instrumental in David's budding career. His first publication was "Electron Microscopy of the Eustachian Tube," in which he graciously listed me as a coauthor. I was also honored when David's son was named for me and became my godson.

David's career resembles a never-ending explosion of fireworks. When I left Ohio to move to Minnesota, David followed my efforts by developing a powerful program in research and attention to otitis media. He helped pioneer scanning electron microscopy, acquired important NIH grants, attracted researchers, and published prolifically. He and Dr. Charles (Charlie) D. Bluestone from Pittsburgh, for example, developed the first international meeting on otitis media, which has promoted and advanced research in multiple disciplines, the results of which have helped thousands of children. David also started the Association for Research in Otolaryngology, the first national and international meeting in the field—with an associated publication for research by MDs and PhDs in otolaryngology and related disciplines. Thousands attend these meetings annually. David's career and research activities continued.

After Ohio State, David was chosen to be the first director of internal research at the NIH. More recently, he was appointed director of research at the well-endowed House Ear Institute in Los Angeles and later became a faculty member at UCLA. It is difficult to consider any more productive and respected researcher in our field of otolaryngology worldwide. Sadly, he passed away in 2018. I was honored to provide a eulogy on his behalf at the cathedral in Los Angeles.

In early 1966, I was approached by a search committee from the University of Minnesota Medical School. Dr. Lawrence R. Boies Sr., one of the respected old guard of otolaryngology, who had been president of most of the national societies, was going to retire as professor and chair of the department. The search committee consisted of eighteen professors (half of whom were chairs of various departments) and Dr. A. B. Baker, an NIH leader of neurology who was professor and chair of the U of M's Neurology Department. Dr. Baker chaired the search committee. Another member of the search committee was Dr. Paul M. Ellwood Jr., a public health physician who conceptualized and coined the term health maintenance organization (HMO). He testified to and sold the idea to Congress. His original concept was reasonable, emphasizing competition among independent health-care providers and institutions, but what eventuated was control by the increasingly large institutions, hospital consortiums, with too few individuals and organizations. That's a common story.

Eighteen individuals were considered for the position. I was thirty-three years old at that time, the youngest department chair in the United States, then and now. For some reason they selected me, and so again I was lucky and grateful for an opportunity. This appointment and this department were considered among the best in the country.

On April 1, 1967, pulling my little U-Haul, I moved to Minnesota to join the University of Minnesota and to live in Minneapolis, a city I'd been told was "a great place to live."

My life and career had transitioned from Michigan to Oregon, back to Michigan, to Germany, to Boston, to Ohio, and now I was moving for the first time to Minnesota, where I was to spend the rest of my career. I didn't know it yet, but I was about to enter the most productive period of my life.

CHAPTER 17

Cold Nights in Minnesota

I am at a four-way stop on a chilly Minnesota night in April. Three other cars sit at the other three stop signs.

The guy on the right waves for the guy on his right to "go."

That guy waves to the guy on his right to "go."

That guy waves to me to "go." I step on the gas and roar through the intersection with my U-Haul. As I look in my rearview mirror, I see one car inch forward at the same time as another. They both slam on their brakes. The third creeps forward cautiously.

Things are going to be different in Minnesota, I can tell already.

I get out of the car to use a pay phone and dial the number I've written on a piece of paper.

"Hello?" He sounds busy.

"Yes, hello," I say. "Dr. Boies?" Dr. Lawrence (Larry) Boies is the current chair of the department I'm to take over. Naturally, I have a few questions.

"We'll talk on Monday," Boies says.

I set up the few belongings I've brought with me from Ohio in the nursing quarters at the university, where I'm to live while my house in Edina is being built. My brother, Tony, a bona fide architect, designed it. Once it's complete, in four or five months, Lynne and the boys will join me here.

My room is dark and small. There's no dog running around, chewing up corners of the furniture. No little-boy shoes or toys to trip over. No scrapping sons to pull off each other before someone gets hurt. There's no Lynne. I feel lonely.

I decide to go for a walk and try to find a little pocket of warmth, maybe even a little Italian joint with wine and good food and familiar-looking people. I wander around and around and people mostly ignore me. Some of the nicer ones greet me with a quick glance and a half smile before turning their heads back down. They seem afraid I'll strike up a conversation. I stumble into a place called the Lincoln Del. Orange lights bounce off the walls and red carpet spreads beneath my feet. It smells like cake and bread. I sit in a booth and listen to the interaction of a Jewish family nearby. I order a Triple Tootsie, which is a platter with three sandwiches, chopped liver, pastrami, and corned beef. I watch and grin as the Jewish grandmother forces more and more food upon her grandson. I eat and stay too long because the restaurant has the warmth of a home. Finally I head back to my room. I'm full. It's quiet. Tomorrow, I'll move my box of temporal bones into my new office and begin again.

After three and a half months, the builder, a big Swede named Swanson, finished my house for fifty thousand dollars. That was a mighty sum in 1967. But I got the house I wanted. It had an unassuming front but a large back that looked over a hilly yard with trees and grass for my boys to run and play with Kapper. By August, the whole family, plus Margaret, moved to Edina. The neighbors politely waved but never invited us for dinner or drinks or "intruded," as they would have considered it.

At work, just as I had done in Boston and Columbus, I had to start my patient-care practice from scratch. Dr. Boies had become the full-time chair of the University of Minnesota's Ear, Nose and Throat (or Otolaryngology) Department in late 1955. He'd also been a member of a private practice group.

When I arrived, Dr. Boies was a bit reserved, but maybe he was just a typical Minnesotan. Later he proved friendly and supportive. But, at first, on some occasions, he'd refer patients to his previous associates in private practice rather than to me. So I started my patient-care practice without patients. I had to grow a practice without much help, as well as figure out fast how to be an administrator at a university. Medical school isn't a good training ground for administrative duties. I had to learn everything through trial and lots of error. I also kept in mind Schuknecht's successes and faults. In particular, I remembered how he taught me everything else: dive in and do. Fast.

The Otolaryngology Department was on the sixth floor of the old Mayo Building at the U of M, and the clinic was on the first floor. The examination chairs were ancient, at least fifty years old. The residents and faculty all used the same facility. Some patients were paying out of pocket, some had insurance coverage, and others were indigent and couldn't pay. It would be years before a new building and more contemporary clinics were built.

For years, the hospital charts had also served as the clinic charts, whether patients were private or not. These charts included handwritten notes by all the physicians, and there could be many at University Hospital, since many patients saw multiple doctors with multiple specialty entries. Imagine these documents! You know how poorly most doctors write, including myself, so trying to decipher the charts, whether in the clinic or in the hospital, was difficult, to say the least. Some of them were six inches or more thick, containing notes scrawled by a dozen different doctors with every kind of shorthand and illegibility.

Among my first tasks as administrator was to propose a method for dictating notes and organizing patient histories and then having them duplicated. One copy stayed at the hospital and one went to my office. I paid for this with my own money because getting funding approval for this kind of advancement would likely have taken seven hundred committees and that many years to process through the university. I'm exaggerating a little bit. But not much. The walls of every university building are made of bureaucracy.

Years later, all medical faculty and university clinics followed suit by developing more decipherable records.

These days, these records are made manifest and organized on the computer. I still have a soft spot for dictating to a secretary, who writes it down and then types it up and creates the electronic record. But, I admit, that is dated technology.

I also established the use of two operating rooms simultaneously, which provided better patient care and better teaching for the residents and fellows, who could get "their hands wet" in the operating room, again, as Schuknecht had taught me. I would work in one room and then move into the second room and modify or finish the otological clinical case. Foreign fellows, both clinical and research, visited from many different countries to observe operations, patient-care techniques, and other aspects of patient care.

Besides teaching residents otolaryngology at the patient bedside in the hospital, in the clinic, and in the operating room, I also lectured to residents and medical students and other health professionals at times.

Remind yourself of the era. Imagine me, the guy who worked a factory job and raised a family through medical school, standing before a room half-populated with hippies and flower children. It's Minnesota. No matter what month, a cluster of tornadoes could drop out of the sky and snow could fall at any moment. But these students are only half dressed, and some of them don't even wear shoes. They put their bare feet up on the backs of seats. Their hair is greasy and smells bad. They read the newspaper while I'm talking. A guy with long dreadlocks in the back is listening to the radio.

The students call me "man"—as in, "Hey, man, is this important?" or "Man, could I borrow a pencil?"

There are race riots on the north side of Minneapolis, and across the country, including in my hometown of Detroit again. Dr. Martin Luther King Jr. speaks about both civil rights and the Vietnam War at the university. He says, "Riots are the language of the unheard."

I didn't have that many years on this new brand of student, but I felt ages older than them. While it was true that I, myself, had never been a stellar student, these kids wore on my last nerve. I lectured to them on this great history, the advancements, the new technologies—all the didactic clinical and scientific information about otology. How dare they not pay attention and take notes? Was respect and preparedness old and out of fashion?

Later, of course, I realized that in every lecture, a more serious student or two was charged with taking notes for everyone so they could all study and pass the exams. I assumed they thought I was boring. I came to believe that maybe I was. Sometimes the "sizzle" is more important than the steak. But at the time, I thought the material was so important that I didn't have to consider my delivery. If they weren't paying attention, I blamed them. I should've been looser and more casual, less formal and stiff, and definitely more personable. Maybe I should have told some jokes to attract their attention and connect with them as humans first.

I learned something from those first years lecturing, though, that subsequently shaped the way I delivered patient care. I have learned and practiced that including more sizzle in both teaching and patient care is important. In patient care, I prioritize getting to know my patients and understanding them as people with families, with friends, with joys and sorrows.

I try to really understand how their hearing loss or their ear pain or vertigo impacts their lives. Building these relationships is good for both of us. The patient builds trust with me. Therefore, they're more at ease when I have to give them a recitation of scientific, clinical facts. They are more at ease when they come in for care. They're more likely to follow up, which means I'm able to keep track of their progress and prevent small problems from escalating into catastrophes. These days, when I meet a new patient, I smile widely, make personal observations, and, since I am now a true Minnesotan, comment on the nice weather (or other personal tidbits) even if the roads are ice rinks or the air is clogged with hot swarms of mosquitoes.

My status at the University of Minnesota Medical School was geographic full-time, just as it had been at Harvard and Ohio State University. This meant the university provided a tiny stipend for being a professor, department chair, researcher, and teacher, and for providing patient care. Then, in accordance with the regents' regulations, doctors had to develop a private practice to support themselves. Geographic full-time is not the same as strict full-time, which is a gig designed for people who enjoy a set salary. I was pleased with my geographic full-time status; I viewed it as an incentive to work hard, see patients, and work closely with medical students.

Though I didn't seek tenure, I was automatically given it. Most, if not all, universities have a policy that all chairs should be tenured. Tenure basically means you have a lifelong job, no matter how productive—or, in some cases, unproductive—you are. Tenure was established for faculty in colleges and universities in the 1930s, mostly to protect them from current and local politics and to protect their freedom of speech and expression. After many decades, cultural and academic climates changed, and tenure deserves new analysis. In my opinion, tenure, in its current form, has long outlived its purpose, especially in medical schools. I have a hypothesis that tenure in all of the universities in America represents many millions of dollars of waste, probably a greater loss to the public than the Mafia recovered during their halcyon days. Maybe someone will investigate tenure in America and write a paperback called *The Tenure Scandal*; I think it would outsell Mario Puzo's *The Godfather*.

CHAPTER 18

The University
of Minnesota

1973. Being a doctor's wife isn't easy in the best of circumstances. The hours are long. The distractions are many. Relocation is common.

In our house, it turns out the task is impossible. All week, I attend to the absorbing demands of my job: building the kind of department the university could be proud of, teaching graduate and medical students, conducting research, soliciting patients, seeing patients, and performing operations. Add conferences, interviews, and travel on top of that—and add that I'm trying with all my might to build a successful private practice. I'm hardly ever home in the house I had built for us. On weekends, I try to squeeze in a trip to the lake near the cabin I bought and the boat I bought. That's what Minnesota doctors are supposed to do, right? Buy lake properties and boats?

It's Friday afternoon. Lynne hasn't seen hide nor hair of me since last Friday, and so she is excited to go to Lake Holcombe in Wisconsin as a family.

"Come on, Dad!" yells Mark. "Drive faster."

He and his brother smile cheerily out the rolled-down windows.

"Huwwy up!" says Steve.

I step on the gas pedal of the station wagon.

When we pull up to our lake house, Lynne and the boys see a relaxing vacation with fishing, swimming, and boating. I see paint peeling off the house, crooked shutters, and poison ivy creeping into the yard. The deer have eaten the shrubs down to the ground and left scat on the sidewalk. The lawn needs to be mowed. A couple of shingles are loose. That tree over there is hanging precariously over the garage. One strong gust of wind and *bam*, down it'll go.

"Dad, let's go boating!" the boys demand. After I unlock the front door, they race in and tear off their clothes.

Lynne pops open a suitcase and digs out their swim trunks. "A boat ride sounds nice," she says.

I glance around the house. There are mouse droppings along the floorboards. The window screen is torn. And something smells off. Probably a septic issue.

"We'll go right after I—" I begin to say.

Lynne's face snaps at me with a "Don't you dare say you're going to do some work" glower.

"—find my swim trunks," I finish.

Her face relaxes. The boys jump around like lunatics.

My boys think I can do anything. I remember thinking my dad could do anything too, when I was their age. They sit patiently, with a little fidgeting, while I try to start the boat's motor.

Rrr-rrrr-rrrr. It goes. Each time, the boys' eyes widen in expectation. *Rrr-rrrr-rrrr.* Nothing.

"Gas," says Lynne.

"That's a good idea." I say. I check the gas tank even though I know it's full. And I try again. *Rrr-rrrr-rrrr.* Finally, the motor chokes out some black smoke and chugs to life. The boys squeal.

"Here we go," I say. We zoom around the lake for a while. I point out a loon with a baby on its back to the boys. We see some jumping fish, a heron on its nest, and an eagle hunting over the water. The boys smile and laugh and climb up and down on Lynne and on me. Out in the middle of the lake, we buckle them into life jackets and let them jump off the sides of the boat into the chilly gray water. Lynne smiles and even laughs out loud a few times. When they're doggy-paddled out, we pull them back up, and she tenderly dries them off. "That was fun, wasn't it?" she says. The boys shake and shiver and giggle through blue lips.

"Let's get back and get some dinner," I say. I feel at ease for the first time in a long time.

The wind picks up a bit on our way back, and the lake ripples into the "walleye chops," making the boat difficult to maneuver. Despite what my boys think about me, I can't do everything. Driving a boat is nothing like driving a car. Unless you're driving a car as the road tips one way and then the other beneath you.

There's another boat near my dock. No matter which way I turn the steering wheel, I am on a direct collision course with it. As we float closer, I see a woman in curlers sunbathing on that boat. I honk my horn. She sits up and waves her arms, as in "Don't crash me." But, it's not as though I'm trying to crash into her. Boats don't have brakes.

Lynne grabs the boys and braces herself. I kill the engine.

We crash into the other boat with a splash and crunch.

"I'm so sorry!" I say.

The woman's very upset. I try to talk to her and calm her down, but she keeps yelling and swearing. We're close enough to the dock so that Lynne can get off the boat and shoo the kids away from the angry lady.

I lean over the boat and inspect the damage. No holes that will sink either of us, just a scrape, scratch, and a dent. The lady in curlers is standing. Her shadow looms over me as she continues her tirade.

"I'll pay for everything," I reassure her.

"You better believe you will! Learn how to drive! Better yet, *don't*. You don't belong anywhere near a boat."

The boys crane their necks to stare at the swearing lady even as Lynne pushes them toward the house.

The rest of our weekend vacation is chilly. It rains. We pack up the kids and head home early on Sunday. Later, we sell the lake house and the boats.

Our life together, Lynne's and mine, unravels. I don't know if what they say about doctors' marriages is true: that they all end. But, it was true in my case. I didn't want to be a statistic. I came from a very traditional Italian family, but my career was difficult for Lynne. Her family insisted she and the boys come back to Detroit. I insisted that she stay in Minnesota so I could take care of her, but Lynne and her family persevered, and I lost.

Lynne takes my sons to Detroit to be near her family, so they can help take care of her and them.

I throw myself into my work more than ever.

* * * * *

Minneapolis is one of the best working cities and has one of the most exciting universities for medical research in the world. In the years before I arrived, the state legislature and Governor Wendell Anderson sought to restructure how schools and local governments were financed because of incredible inequalities between wealthy neighborhoods and towns versus poor ones. Those reforms led to a revitalization called the "Minnesota Miracle of 1971." Governor Anderson even found himself holding a walleye in a *Time* magazine cover photo in August 1973. The headline read "The Good Life in Minnesota." Building on the momentum of the day, a time of learning from the past, creating innovative solutions, and applying them even when they were risky, I found many opportunities to bring improvement to the "crown jewel" of the state: the University of Minnesota.

The U of M and its hospitals were then largely occupied by professors who emphasized research and teaching, to the relative diminishment of patient care. One of the acute challenges of my earlier years at the university was an inadequate population of patients for teaching patient care. Some faculty with MDs resorted to research and teaching only, while others had a modest clinic in which they saw patients, but most of their time was spent in research, teaching, and administration.

I decided my strategy to address the problem would be to recruit and build the best faculty and staff. In 1967, as is the situation now, the university had four teaching hospitals where the residents rotated. The University of Minnesota Hospital on campus is at the center, and it's the most active in terms of patient care, research, and teaching. Besides the key professors, Dr. Frank Lassman (audiology), Dr. Dixon Ward (research), Dr. Jack Duvall, (clinical and research), important contributions to teaching were provided by Dr. Jerry Hilger and his group in Saint Paul and Dr. Bob Priest and his associates in Minneapolis. The other hospitals in the university system are Hennepin County General Hospital (now called Hennepin County Medical Center), St. Paul-Ramsey Hospital (now called Regions Hospital), and the Veterans Administration Hospital, and in 1967 none had full-time ENT staff. I hired Dr. Larry Boies Jr., Harvard-trained, to head up ENT at St. Paul-Ramsey Hospital. I hired Dr. Henry L. Williams, a lifelong smoker who tugged an oxygen tank wherever he went, to practice at the VA in Minneapolis. He had previously been the chairman of otolaryngology at the Mayo Clinic.

I tried to hire an Italian for an appointment at Hennepin County General. A guy named Dr. Thomas C. Calcaterra. Tommy's dad owned the only funeral parlor in my old Detroit neighborhood. But he got scooped by a Hollywood hospital, so I put Dr. Robert (Bob) Mathog from Duke in at that post. Each new hire brought an excellent reputation, which attracted residency applicants in the hundreds from all over the world. I believed then, and still do, that all people have value and bring value to their communities when afforded the opportunity to make a difference. I believed then, and still do, that a diversity of backgrounds, experiences, and points of view bring creative thinking and ingenuity to research and its applications.

People all over the world bleed and feel the same and want to improve their lives, their families' lives, and the lives of others. For that reason, although I could have filled our residency positions, six per year for five years of training, with graduates of the U of M's medical school, most with blond hair and blue eyes and with surnames like Johnson, Peterson, and Larson, I solicited excellent international candidates.

Among so many other wonderful people, one in particular comes to mind: Dr. Jake Guzowski who was number one among his graduating class of at least two thousand at the National Autonomous University of Mexico. He was accepted, trained, and became the best ENT doctor in Costa Rica. Years later, when I attended an academic conference he arranged there, he picked me up from the airport. It was a shock to see the "kid" I'd trained all those years before, the one with a mop of shiny black hair, now bald from chemo treatments and dying. He died much too young from glioblastoma multiforme, a malignant tumor of the brain, the very same as my mother's. I'll never forget him. My heart still hurts when I think about that young man.

I often reflected on my own journey as the son of immigrants, poor immigrants with very little formal education, and I often remembered my father's complete devotion to making sure I received an education—not only to graduate high school, but to become a doctor. What had made him so bold? Such a dream could have never come true if he'd stayed in Italy. It was the promise of America that he absorbed when he arrived and that he instilled in me. Now, at the University of Minnesota, I made it my mission to ensure that other, seemingly unexpected, people had the same opportunity.

I needed to get more money coming in to pay for all these new hires and the research programs we were trying to build. Only by sticking his neck out can a turtle move forward, and identify and adapt to avoid dangers. Whether recruiting faculty, applying for grants, or developing other areas for progress, this was also true of the Department of Otolaryngology: we were sticking our necks out. The goal was for successes to supersede any failures or disappointments. While patient care was an important and growing component of our program, my next major goals were also important: enhancing and building a strong academic program, accomplishable through research and education.

When I joined the U of M, it was already considered one of the best departments in the United States, but I wanted to strengthen its existing core academic base. The way to do this was to acquire grants for research, especially NIH grants. I and other faculty members wrote a lot of grant proposals for considerable funds, which became the main source of funding for the department's development. When I didn't have time for grant writing, I delegated the responsibility.

A friend, Dr. John E. Bordley, who was professor and chair of otolaryngology at Johns Hopkins University and an active consultant to NIH, called and said, "You have a good crew at the University of Minnesota. Why don't you apply for an NIH program grant?"

I'd already acquired research grants from NIH, the Deafness Research Foundation, the American Otological Society, the Hartford Foundation, and many others so I thought we should apply. But, because I was personally swamped with work and administrative duties, I asked our most respected researcher to lead the program grant and serve as principal investigator. The principal investigator needs to facilitate and organize a team that works together. I came to realize that I didn't stress "work together" enough.

This person was a very good scientist, but he was an independent worker. And he assumed that others worked in the same way: alone. So he asked many of the investigators on the grant to write up their own individual sections for a proposal called "Mechanisms of Sensorineural Hearing Loss," which included research in the disciplines of psychoacoustics, psychophysics, otopathology, research audiology, biostatistics, speech pathology, electron microscopy, and more, with the otopathology laboratory being central to the grant.

Sensorineural hearing loss is the most common type of deafness and hearing loss; it affects more than forty million people. We could have really used that grant money to study this phenomenon. Unfortunately, there was no collaboration, cohesion, or sense of teamwork in the creation of the proposal. On top of that, the site visit was a disaster. In the blast of a Minnesota freeze-over, the distinguished grant reviewers arrived. No one greeted them at the airport. No one waited for them when the taxicab dropped them off on the street corner. Once they finally made their way to the hospital, their faces were chapped and so were their last nerves. Needless to say, we weren't funded.

That rejection didn't deter me, though. Failure is an important component of success. Failure forces learning and new actions. After reviewing the rejected proposal, it was clear to me that rather than one cohesive proposal, it read like a collection of disparate ideas. I took over the role of principal investigator on the second attempt at the grant. In the same way car factory workers, though independently expert at their job, work together to contribute to one, ultimate product, I organized my researchers to do the same. When the site team arrived, I served as chauffeur and tour guide and exercised the same happy hosting skills my mother had shown to those Italian POWs all those years before. We got the grant.

The reputation of the department as a research institution grew, especially after I helped develop another large program grant proposal titled "Pathogenesis of Otitis Media." We would study etiology of the disease from many angles—otopathology, biochemistry, electron microscopy, microbiology, auditory physiology, pediatric research, molecular biology, genetics, biostatistics, and so on. These two grants each provided a million dollars per year for research.

A year or so later when David Lim and I served on the council of the National Institute on Deafness and Other Communication Disorders, part of the NIH, we encouraged others to apply for and acquire program grants in otitis media as well. Some were funded. Some were not.

The grants awarded to the U of M, including those awarded to other members of the faculty, helped develop the department's status in research and education. Not only the medical school but the departmental faculty demonstrated that they could give much more than they could receive in terms of financial support. It's a little-known fact that departments in the University of Minnesota Medical School (and other major public universities) receive scant support from state legislatures, so they need to raise money through patient care, grants, and, if possible, endowed funds.

Research in its various forms leads to a better understanding of the myriad diseases that cause deafness and other common ear problems. Research leads to better methods of diagnosis and treatment of ear diseases, as well as diseases of the head and neck. Research activities and funding strengthen academic programs. The second way to build academic strength is through post-graduate education through residencies and fellowships. Training otolaryngologists who seek additional surgical and research experience enhances the development of their careers. Later when they join university faculties, they teach others in patient care and research. The positive effects ripple outward forever, like a rock dropped in a still pool of water.

Recollecting my years of research in the temporal bone laboratory in the repurposed funeral home on East Grand Boulevard in Detroit, where I accomplished assembly-line procedures in the style of Henry Ford's methodology for manufacturing cars, I thought a similar principle could apply to training residents in the environment of a graduate school. Why? Because life is short, and because an individual can accomplish more in a day or in an evening than he or she thinks possible.

The faculty and I added another level of rigor to our residents' training. Along with their residency, they would concomitantly acquire a master of science or PhD within the five years of training. At first, the faculty was hesitant to accept my idea, but they came to see the wisdom of it. I wasn't necessarily interested in the type of degree participants pursued. In fact, I hoped to see a diversity of concentrations. It was the learning and the work ethic that were most important to me. I've often said, "I don't care if you have an MD, DDS, PhD, LLD, or MS—the degree you should get is a j-o-b." I believe this was, during my tenure and to date, the only program of its sort in the United States.

I was hopeful our residents would not only become excellent otolaryngologists but also, by promoting research and education, practice tomorrow's medicine and not yesterday's. I wanted them to go on to train others based on the same principles, and many did. In addition, a number of our former residents and fellows became community leaders and leaders of medical societies.

During my full-time tenure at the University of Minnesota from 1967 to 1985, we trained a number of PhDs and more than thirty-five students who acquired a master's degree. During that period, we trained most of the ENT doctors in Minnesota, and they had better otologic training than most post-residency otology-neurotology fellows generally have. We trained people who went on to become world-renowned university otolayrngologists. We trained people who became world-famous ear specialists and people who ran important institutes.

While I very much enjoyed my work with research and patients and training residents, I had to make a personal and professional change. The bureaucracy of the university felt somewhat stifling, and I wondered if I couldn't make more of an impact on town-gown health from outside the institution.

Generally faculty members of associate professorship rank or higher work hard to publish their scientific studies, acquire NIH grants, and energize their faculty colleagues and their chair to recommend them for tenure to the medical school's promotions committee. But after achieving tenure, I noted that too many of them were less productive in research and teaching, and some were even counterproductive. These sorts of problems weren't unique to our program. In one case, a tenured member of the faculty didn't show up for months. In another case,

I witnessed blatant criminality, stealing products from a funded NIH grant.

Seems like a firing would be in order, right? Nope. Not so fast. Universities have due-process committees full of deliberations and investigations that go on and on and on. They absorbed way too much of my time as chair. The case of the stolen NIH money went on so long that, finally, the tenured faculty member found herself with the opportunity to retire with no penalty whatsoever.

Think of the time, money, and brainpower wasted on this bureaucratic problem.

At the end of 1984, I knew it was time for a change, so I decided to leave my full-time faculty position and give up my tenure. But I didn't want to abandon the university. So I set out to support the department from the private sector. My university salary at that time was forty thousand dollars, plus what I could supplement through private practice. I could have been paid more and been less productive—and, because of my tenure, I could have earned much more until my very senior years. But this approach was not in my DNA. Finally, I was going to answer my father's question, "When will you get a real job?"

"Now, Pa. Now I will get a real job—according to your definition."

CHAPTER 19

Ingenuity and Invention

This child isn't impressed with this procedure. He seems poised to kick really hard. His mother has a wrinkle between her eyebrows, and her mouth is pinched so tight her lips are white.

"Now this won't hurt a bit," the audiologist says to the boy at the same time the nurse offers in a singsong voice, "It only hurts a little bit."

But this is not going well.

"I'm only going to pour water into your ear and then check your eyes," the audiologist says, grinning widely.

The child, a bright chap of twelve years old, clamps his hands over his ears and screams, "Nooooooo!" He's a recurrent patient. He has dizziness. And this test, called a caloric stimulation (as part of videonystagmography, or VNG), will help me understand why.

The mother has her arms around her child. She says, "Can't you just give us an antibiotic, and we'll be on our way?"

"I'm afraid not," the audiologist says, as sympathetically as he can. "Now, hold his head as still as possible." She looks at him skeptically, with one eyebrow arched up like a mean cat. The audiologist fixes himself in front of the child so he can observe his eyes once the water stimulates his inner ear and changes its temperature. The boy's eyes should dart involuntarily back and forth, a response called nystagmus. If they don't, then there's damage to the balance part of the inner ear.

The nurse prepares to gently pour the water into the little guy's ear. He begins to kick and wail. Mom puts one arm over his legs to keep him still.

"OK, here we go!" the audiologist says.

Mom holds his head and clamps down his legs with one of her own. The nurse begins pouring the water into his ear. The little guy flings his arm toward the source of his misery and sends the water apparatus flying across the room.

Start over.

"OK, here we go," the audiologist says, more muted this time.

Mom straightjackets kid. Nurse pours water. Kid wails. Eyes dart back and forth just as they're supposed to. "Good, good," the audiologist says. Nurse gets a towel and helps turn the little guy on his side so the water drains from his ear. He's crying and red faced. He tells the audiologist that he hates him. He tells his mother he hates her too. Her eyes well up with tears. He sobs into her chest.

After a while, he calms down.

"There we go," the audiologist says. He pats his shoulder. "All better. Just one more ear to go."

There's got to be a better way to do this, I think.

* * * * *

Practicing clinical otology-neurotology requires the use of a variety of specialized microscopic instruments and tools. I found that the tools available were generally fine, but that I had to create additional tools, instruments, and prostheses to better help my patients. After I practiced using them myself, I began teaching other doctors how to use them.

When I worked with Harold Schuknecht prior to serving in the army, I had an opportunity to use instruments he designed. Then, while serving in Nuremberg, I had to design and develop my own innovative instruments with a set of dental tools and a Bunsen burner. Over the decades, as we learned more about different diseases of the ear, more tools had to be developed to accommodate microscopic otologic surgery.

I collaborated with various surgical instrument supply houses, such as Storz, Richards Company, Xomed, and especially, V. Mueller, a leading maker of instruments for surgery. William Merz, chief of instrument development at V. Mueller, was a legend in the field of instrument design. I had the privilege of knowing him and working with him on a variety of products.

We created canal knives with replaceable blades. These became a Paparella #1 and a #2 canal knife. We also improved another instrument called the duckbill knife elevator, which is used to elevate the ear canal in tympanoplasty procedures. Later, many other surgical companies replicated our ideas.

Another improvement we contributed to ear surgery was inspired out of a procedural issue I noticed while operating. Instruments for surgery were always sterilized in one tray and then served to the surgeon, by the scrub nurse, from another tray. It seemed to me that we could combine these two efforts so the delicate instruments could be sterilized and then made appropriately available for surgery during the procedures. Thus, we developed an instrument-holder that was sterilizable and would stand upright so the scrub nurse could carefully select the instruments at the doctor's request for various aspects of the procedure.

Ventilation tubes are commonly used for children who have constant ear infections due to accumulation of fluids in the middle ear. If less-invasive medical care isn't enough, and the child continues to have deafness and fluid in the ear, then the fluid has to be removed. A ventilation tube is inserted to provide aeration to the middle ear and drain fluid from the dysfunctional Eustachian tube, the cause of the problem in the first place. We were the first to develop ventilation tubes using Silastic, which is silicon rubber.

Silastic is a very malleable, inert material used widely in cardiac surgery, breast implants, and for many other purposes throughout the body. The tubes were designed uniquely with a special notched inner flange to make insertion easier, an outer flange, and a tag to make it simple to remove in the clinic. Also, for the first time, we created optional sizes. One larger size was used for obstinate cases of recurrent effusion in the middle ear such as mucoid otitis media, while the other was used more routinely.

During that era, I fancied myself a scientist and a doctor. I didn't emphasize my clinical activities or development of these tools. Boy, was I dumb.

A gentleman visited me from Milwaukee. He liked the tubes I designed, and he wanted to get companies to manufacture and sell them. He asked for a patent, and, stupidly, I gave it to him. I handed it over. I gave away my patent.

Eventually, these Paparella tubes were sold by all the companies making surgical instruments—and, years later, that man sued several of those companies and collected millions of dollars retroactively because he felt he hadn't gotten enough of the royalties! *He* hadn't gotten enough royalties. Can you believe that?

Adding insult to injury, I was compelled to attend legal depositions on a gratis basis, while he was awarded a significant percentage of all previous sales and collected a huge number of dollars.

I obviously should have kept and signed my own patent. I wanted to kick myself when I thought about all the money that could have been used to support research in otopathology, which has always been a constant struggle. All the tools and equipment I designed and developed (with others and engineers in some cases) were done without a patent. Not too smart.

At the start of the new millennium, I developed another set of Paparella tubes with different designs for slightly different purposes. One of these we use commonly, called the Paparella 2000 Type 2 ear ventilation tube. Incidentally, these ventilation tubes are not only used in children but in adults who have certain types of diseases and effusions of the middle ear, often associated with microscopic reconstructive ear operations, such as tympanoplasty.

Around 1966, I noted that many children and adults with normal eardrums or with perforations of their eardrums and dizziness couldn't tolerate the electronystagmography (ENG) test, which required pouring relatively large amounts of very cold and very warm water into the ear to measure possible abnormalities in the vestibular labyrinth, the balance part of the inner ear. It was difficult and painful for the child or adult, and the test couldn't be used on many occasions, such as when there was current ear disease, including infections in the mastoid cavity or perforations of the eardrum. At that time, there was something called a Dundas-Grant device, but it was rarely used. The Dundas-Grant apparatus was a metal coil with a rubber bulb at the end. You would spray ethyl chloride on the coil and squeeze the bulb, and cooled air entered the ear to stimulate the caloric test without using water. This method of using air instead of water appealed to me, so I worked with a firm in Chicago and over many, many prototypes over many, many years, we finally developed an ENG machine—and later a videonystagmography (VNG) machine—that used air-caloric stimulation, hot and cold, instead of hot and cold water poured from buckets. This machine became a valuable tool, not only to otolaryngologists but to audiologists worldwide. Patients, especially children and anxious adults, tolerated the tests much better.

I encountered a familiar problem. After working with my staff and engineers, an equipment company in Chicago helped me develop the air-caloric machine, which sells for thousands of dollars; again we didn't receive any royalties from the sales. The company was going to throw us a bone by at least putting the name of the University of Minnesota on the machine, but then the owner of the company, who had made the promise, died in an airplane crash. A different company took over and distributed and sold the product without any acknowledgment. During those days, I wasn't an entrepreneur, but *slowly* I was starting to learn my lesson.

Another device we created was an electronic masker, which makes it possible to measure the hearing in individual ears by masking the other. Audiograms are important and critical to practicing otology. They provide functional information regarding hearing loss, which correlates to decibels of loss relative to various frequencies. Audiology also measures discrimination, which relates to the patient's ability to understand speech. It also measures tympanometric information that tells us about the pressure or lack thereof behind the eardrum, which can indicate Eustachian tubal function or dysfunction. While these tests require accurate machines, they're subjective, because the patient has to respond to sounds. Patients can respond differently according to subjective parameters.

Therefore, before surgery it's critical that we check each patient—for example, one who has a conductive loss—using tuning-fork testing and a masker to eliminate the opposite ear so we know we're measuring the ear tested and not the opposite side, or a crossover effect. It would be a mistake to operate on an ear for the incorrect hearing loss. Masking is essential.

The masker that was available before the electronic version, called the Bárány Box, was very old-fashioned and made a huge rattling noise in the patient's ear. It was discomforting, and children couldn't stand it. The electronic masker made by Starkey Laboratoires is much more bearable, provides a large shooshing sound like white noise, and is accepted more readily by children and adults to make certain that the hearing loss is conductive and suitable for surgery.

CHAPTER 20

Publish, or It Didn't Happen

It's January 1975, a few days after the worst blizzard I've ever seen, and already everyone is calling it the storm of the century. It came upon the city like a wall of fog. In the southern part of the state, cows froze standing up. More than a dozen deaths have been tallied. I've noticed that storms bring out the best in Minnesotans. Your Minnesota neighbors won't say a word to you all year, but once the snow starts flying, their faces change. Suddenly, they're standing at your doorstep with shovels, and they're behind your car pushing to get you out of a drift. "Some weather!" they cheer, clapping their mitted hands on your back.

Today, Bud Grant and the Minnesota Vikings and their Purple People Eaters defensive line are playing the Pittsburgh Steelers in the Super Bowl. But the lead story of every news station is the weather.

My phone rings. It's Pa. "How are you, my son?"

"Good, Dad. It snowed here a whole bunch. It's been in the news. Did you see?"

"No. We're busy. Making gnocchi and lasagna and spaghetti and raviolis with sausage."

My mouth waters. "Who's going to eat all that?"

In the background, I hear the distinct clink of pots and pans in a kitchen that has been reawakened with activity. A while ago, my father, once again with the help of relatives, began corresponding with an Italian woman living in Canada. They hit it off pretty well. So he went there, met her, married her, and brought her to Detroit. She was a great cook, having made food for many Italian weddings.

Faustina dotes on our father. She stuffs him with pasta until he fills out his shirts. She can make a delicious dish out of whatever is lying around, and she does. Including my nephews' pet rabbit that he left unattended in the backyard. Faustina had no idea it was Richie's beloved pet. So into the pot it went for Sunday dinner. Josephine's little Richie was horrified.

"He'll get over it," I told Josephine.

"I know. We did," she joked. She was recalling the way Ma dispatched chickens and turkeys for our own meals. We agreed that those memories hadn't scarred us for life.

"How's the wine coming along?" I ask Pa.

"Oh good." I can hear Faustina talking to my dad in Italian.

He responds to her in Italian. He laughs and tells her to make lots and lots because he's built up an appetite.

"OK, Pa. I better go."

"Is everything going good, my son?"

I can't speak for a moment. After Lynne took the kids to live near her parents and siblings, I sold the house and moved into an apartment. Really, I live at work. I even eat, shower, and sometimes catnap there. The apartment is just a place where I have my bills sent.

"Yeah, I'm all right, Pa. I gotta go."

"You need a wife." I hear Faustina giggling like a schoolgirl in the background. "And a real job!"

"Bye, Pa," I say and hang up. The minute I hang up, the phone rings again.

"Hello?" I say. I'm expecting it to be Dad. Maybe he forgot something.

"Hey!" It's a friend who's been nagging me to go out. "A bunch of us are going out to listen to some music tonight."

"No, I'm not—"

"I'm not taking no for an answer. You need to get out of that apartment and quit moping. Life goes on, friend."

I look around my little apartment. There's a dead plant in the window and empty takeout boxes and bags on the counter. I can hear the refrigerator humming. I have to get out of here. "Yeah. OK. Yeah. I'll go."

* * * * *

A few years after my separation and divorce from Lynne, I purchased a 1902 home from the contrabassoon-player for the Minnesota Symphony Orchestra. He and his wife didn't get along and were separating. For some reason, the wife had installed sixteen Airedale terriers in cages in the master bedroom. Think about the lingering smell. The dogs had also destroyed all the grass in the backyard and created an odor the neighbors found very disagreeable. Although the house had lovely historical elements—including beautiful stained-glass windows and natural Philippine mahogany—it needed a lot of work. The basement floor was dirt, the original oil furnace and radiators were defective and leaked, and the canine odor suffusing the house couldn't be cured by opening windows because the smell from the backyard was just as bad. I moved in and got busy. Over the years, I did three major rehabilitations to make it a warm, comfortable, antique home with some contemporary additions.

When I wasn't at the hospital or fixing up my house, I could sometimes be strong-armed by my pals into going out and listening to music, particularly at a nightclub in Edina. The bandleader and his band members were all born in Italy, and they had a unique and beautiful echo-reverberating European sound. I became friends with the bandleader. He introduced me to Rebecca Hendrickson, a pretty blonde. She was interesting and smart, and we dated. Soon we were married by a judge in his office. But work still took up most of my time, and I wasn't a very attentive husband. Too many important and exciting advancements were occurring at the hospital. When it came to entrepreneurship and my personal life, I was a pretty slow learner.

I also was writing a lot. You can't make good use of research if nobody knows about it. What good would it be to keep my discoveries to myself? So I felt in my core that it was part of my responsibility to publish. If I didn't, I thought, it was almost as if the research never happened.

The first book I got involved with was while I was at Ohio State, *The Atlas of Ear Surgery*. Over time, four editions were published, the first in 1968, then later editions in 1980, 1986, and 1989. The book provided pictures and line drawings, and it was easy to understand. It included brief descriptions of the diseases and the relevant surgical techniques. I worked with the book's artist in the operating room on multiple occasions, so she could actually see the surgical procedures, using an observation tube, and then render images of them for this easy-to-follow atlas, the first of its kind. Dr. William H. (Bill) Saunders and I were the initial coauthors; Dr. Andrew Miglets, who was a resident at that time and later a faculty member, became a coauthor and revised later editions. The book was well received by all; it was an easy guide to use in temporal bone dissection, teaching ear surgeons how to dissect on normal temporal bones before they perform microscopic surgery on a living patient. It also provided clear and concise descriptions of surgical techniques for ear surgery, including skull-base surgery. In subsequent years and with other colleagues, we helped develop other atlases of ear surgery.

Most of the publications documenting my research findings originated from the Otopathological Research Laboratory (the Human Temporal Bone Research Laboratory) at the University of Minnesota. There are a few published research contributions I consider particularly pioneering and noteworthy. One is "Sensorineural Hearing Loss in Chronic Otitis Media and Mastoiditis," published in 1970, where this common complication of otitis media was first described. In patients who have chronic ear infections, the infection may spread to the inner ear and cause sensorineural hearing loss or dizziness. This can even occur in small children; a child will get ear infections and will have not only hearing loss and pressure but also perhaps problems with balance or dizziness. If we remove the fluid pressure and place a ventilation tube, the child no longer bumps into the walls at school or runs into the doorframe of his bedroom. And he can hear better too. This publication led to multiple research studies from our laboratories, and resulted in international meetings that were held regularly in Umea, Sweden. Eventually it resulted in an NIH grant funded in association with Dr. Steven S. Juhn as principal investigator.

Another important study and publication was "Cellular Events Involved in Middle Ear Fluid Production," researched for the first time in animals, which translates immediately to research for humans. Importantly, the continuum of the otitis medias was first described, showing how an early type of otitis media can lead to serious chronic otitis media and chronic mastoiditis characterized by a tumor-like tissue. We found that cellular events causing the development of chronic otitis media include involvement by the space below the epithelial lining of the middle ear. The epithelium can produce pus, serous fluid, and mucoid fluid in otitis media that sometimes leads to the development of pathologic tissue.

Children's ear infections or inflammations can lead to many other problems during adulthood, such as perforation of the tympanic membrane, atelectasis in which the tympanic membrane collapses and thins out, ossicular erosion or fixation, and so on.

Another important research study published was titled "Chronic Silent Otitis Media." We found that serious pathologic conditions can exist behind an intact tympanic membrane. All of the publications in the world, even to date, describe chronic otitis media and chronic mastoiditis as requiring a perforation and otorrhea (drainage) from the ear. Our studies indicated that is clearly not the case. Some serious ear diseases can be silent, i.e., symptomless, before they internalize to the inner ear, where they can cause sensorineural hearing loss or dizziness—or even sometimes spread to the intracranial space, as we found in a number of pediatric temporal bones. These children died of *Haemophilus* meningitis following chronic silent otitis media.

Ménière's disease has plagued people since the dawn of man. But we're only recently beginning to understand it. Along with Vincent van Gogh, Jonathan Swift—the satirist and poet best known for "A Modest Proposal," an essay in which he wryly suggests the Irish poor sell their children to the rich for food—suffered from it as much as anyone. Like Van Gogh, Swift suffered in a time when the disease was mischaracterized as melancholy, epilepsy, and fits. He seemed to understand the nature of his disease though. Toward the end of his life, he pointed to a dying tree and said, "I shall be like that tree. I shall die at the top." It is possible he lived with the disease for most of his life, including his youth, as many historians note that he had bouts of vertigo and nausea as a very young man.

I've devoted significant time to studying Ménière's disease, including its pathology and pathogenesis. Some have called the disease "glaucoma of the inner ear," and I have used this description to explain the condition to patients too. In research publications, we described the histopathology of how Ménière's disease can be associated either causally or coincidentally with other diseases such as chronic otitis media, trauma, or otosclerosis. The prestigious medical journal *The Lancet* asked me to describe this dreadful disease, which I did with my coauthor Dr. Hamed Sajjadi; we included both research and clinical data. Over the years and sometimes with other faculty, I have published 148 publications relating to Ménière's disease (out of 720 publications total).

Ménière's disease, which has confounded many in otology, was thought not to occur in children, but our study proves otherwise. It's often considered largely unilateral, meaning it affects only one ear. Bilateral Ménière's disease was thought to be very infrequent, but this study and other related studies show its presence in both ears is much more common; bilaterality can occur in 50 percent of patients over time. This fact should be considered when destructive procedures are offered, as no physician dares or wants to destroy both ears. We were first to discuss the anatomical considerations of the endolymphatic sac, including a deep sigmoid sinus and a reduced Trautmann's triangle (a bony partition that separates the mastoid from the posterior intracranial space) and other anatomical anomalies. The anomalies are part of the causation and therefore important in the treatment of Ménière's disease, especially treatment by endolymphatic sac-enhancement surgery (ESE), a procedure I developed.

Importantly, some patients who had ESE, about 7–8 percent of them, years later will have developed all the symptoms of incapacitating Ménière's disease once again, and thus we have the option of using destructive procedures, either chemical or physical, or a conservative procedure. (Destructive procedues include chemical labyrinthectomy or physical labyrinthectomy, or vestibular nerve section which is an intracranial or brain procedure.) We have, in hundreds of cases, done revisions of endolymphatic sac surgery and have found scar tissue invading the mastoid and the endolymphatic sac. Correcting that has led to hundreds of patients who continue to be well to date without having to resort to destructive procedures. We remove fibrous tissue and perform an endolymphatic sac revision so the patient can have a normal life.

Another publication described and discussed my method of ESE, for intractable vertigo and other disabling symptoms in patients with Ménière's disease, an operation I have used in almost three thousand patients. The majority of these patients have benefited greatly.

For years I've studied patients and human temporal bones in an attempt to understand the causes, pathology, and pathogenesis of Ménière's disease. Many other otologists continue to refer to it as idiopathic, which means "I don't know anything about its cause." Years ago, though, I described the cause of Ménière's disease as multifactorial inheritance, which I still believe to be true. For the vast majority of patients, the cause is genetic. The pathogenesis appears due to endolymph malabsorption and the cause of symptoms is due to chemical and physical micro events. So far as I know, I was the first to describe the cause as genetically induced. The publication at a collegium meeting was more than forty years ago and repeated at a more recent international meeting on Ménière's disease.

Moreover, I found that upwards of 20 percent of my patients had a positive family history of the disease (as common, if not more so, than otosclerosis, a known genetic deafness disease) and since my first presentation, more than eighty basic science publications have studied and demonstrated chromosomal abnormalities in Ménière's disease. Unfortunately, the responsible gene has not yet been identified.

In addition, while performing my method of ESE for patients who are incapacitated with vertigo; deafness; pressure; tinnitus and loudness intolerance, I observed almost everyone had congenital abnormalities. The sigmoid sinus is a large vein in the mastoid that transfers blood from the brain and then to the jugular vein, and lastly to the heart, and in almost every patient with intractable Ménière's disease, it was located in a deep medial anterior position which reduces or eliminates Traut-man's Triangle.

Every five years, an international symposium on Ménière's disease is held. The most recent was in Rome, Italy, where I was a guest of honor—a privilege I enjoyed at two previous such international meetings. I was there to describe the genetic cause and pathogenesis of Ménière's. My bonus prize was a personal meeting with the pope.

Studies in animals and humans have had a greater clinical relevance than bench-oriented research in terms of helping patients with the many disturbing and incapacitating otological diseases. No man is an island, and the research I discuss above—and my other research that isn't outlined here—almost always included my respected and capable colleagues and fellows. Many of these people continue conducting good research and contributing important publications. I worked hard to get the "right" people in the "right" positions, and my belief that the University of Minnesota ought to be a premier research institution was contagious. The department was prolific in publications.

* * * * *

In 1968, I was approached by the publisher W.B. Saunders Company, the leading medical publisher, to consider a replacement publication for *Diseases of the Nose, Throat and Ear,* edited by Dr. Chevalier Jackson and his son Dr. Chevalier L. Jackson, the leading textbook of its time. I nearly choked, recalling that it had been the only thing I studied before passing my board exams.

"Me?" I said. "Are you sure?"

"Yes, of course," the editor responded. "Don't you know how well respected your work is, doctor?"

I didn't, actually. But I agreed to the project, and I got to work with my coeditor and coauthor, Dr. Donald Shumrick, a friend who was professor and chair of otolaryngology at the University of Cincinnati.

Otolaryngology as a title for the book was not adequate to cover the profession and its activities. The term *ear, nose, and throat*, or *ENT*, was less accurate and inclusive. So I suggested a three-volume text titled *Ear, Head, and Neck*. I suggested that the first volume should be dedicated to the basic sciences of the specialty. No other textbook in medicine prior to that time—or, to my knowledge, since—had devoted one whole volume to basic sciences as its own specialty. Everybody was initially skeptical but they later agreed. Volume I was *Basic Sciences*, volume two was *Otology*, and volume three was *Head and Neck Surgery*. For the third edition, a fourth volume on plastic and reconstructive surgery was added.

At that time, 1971, there were about six thousand otolaryngologists in the United States. W.B. Saunders felt if we could sell three thousand sets (i.e., nine thousand books), the publication would be a huge success, recognizing that these volumes are large and expensive. Instead, more than nine thousand sets, or almost thirty thousand books, were sold in the United States and worldwide. Further, we were copied in many other countries, often without permission of the publisher. Though we had only modest expectations, the volumes became a "bible." The first edition was published in 1973, the second in 1980, and the third edition (with its additional fourth volume) in 1991.

Another publication to highlight was the *Yearbook of Otolaryngology Head and Neck Surgery*. The *Yearbook* was first developed by Dr. Land, professor and chair of the University of Chicago, in 1896. As chief of ENT and ophthalmology, his first books were dedicated to those specialties. Eventually the book was published for more than thirty-five specialties. It was very widely read by the medical community. Editors of the *Yearbook* included giants in the field of otolaryngology, and I joined them for the field of otology in 1971. Our job was to review and discuss, favorably or unfavorably, all publications that were considered significant from all the major journals of otolaryngology in the United States and other countries. That's a lot of reading, but what a wonderful opportunity to glimpse at all the incredible research and work being done all over the world for the betterment of human health and quality of life.

More recently, in 2019, a two-volume textbook entitled *Paparella's Otolaryngology Head and Neck Surgery*, was also, reluctantly, published. Designed for an international audience, I wanted to call it *Global Otolaryngology Head and Neck Surgery*, but my two respected and capable co-editors, Dr. Da Costa (professor and chairman in Brazil) and Dr. Fagan (professor and chairman in South Africa) and the publisher insisted that it bear its current title. Three hundred expert professionals, including many of my past students, contributed chapters. I believe many of my colleagues will say, "Gee, I thought he retired . . . or died!" But we persist.

* * * *

And, yes, alongside all this reading, writing, editing, organizing, and working, I was again a newlywed, to Rebecca. At first Becky didn't want children, but soon she changed her mind. Maybe she grew lonely in my constant absence. So in 1982 we made arrangements through a former resident and associate of mine from Chile. From there, we brought three-month-old Lisa home to Minnesota and adopted her into our family. Lisa was a bright-eyed bundle of warmth. A complete joy.

Pretty quickly, however, it became obvious that I might have rushed into things with Becky. Even though we didn't always get along, we tried to make things work. Eventually, though, we separated and divorced. So, again, I was a bachelor. I was on my own again on the home front. Guess what I did?

I worked.

CHAPTER 21

The Board

Dr. Boies looks like he stepped out of Norman Rockwell's "The Doctor and the Doll," the painting of a family doctor examining a little girl's baby doll. As I rap lightly on his office door, he's bent over his desk, handwriting bills to his patients. Over the years, he's warmed up to me.

"Come in, Dr. Paparella," he says. But he doesn't look up from his document. He reviews it, signs it, and then greets me with a smile. Despite the impression conveyed by his modest office, Dr. Boies is a national leader in politics, important committees, and the American Board of Otolaryngology.

"You wanted to see me?"

He leans back and crosses his fingers on his belly. "Yes. I want to talk to you." He pauses. "I like what you're doing around here."

There's very little gratitude in this world. Doctoring can be thankless. Administrating is like walking around with a bull's-eye on your back. Moving a whole group of people toward the same common goals has been one of the most challenging undertakings of my life. You have to lead and take risks, but in doing so, you put your own reputation on the line. When things go right, nobody notices. When things go wrong, the blame is on me.

So many egos are at play. Doctors and staff aren't peons I can order around without backlash. Some of them are traditionalists, who prefer every little thing be done exactly the way it's been done for the past fifty years. Some of them want to race to "the next big thing" before proper research. I have to figure out how to prod the turtles and rein in the hares, all the while attending to my own students and patients. Every individual requires a certain kind of leadership style from me to succeed. Some need a coach. Some need a confidant. Some need a general. I'm something slightly different for everyone, but I still have to maintain my own dignity and be myself.

No wonder I'm single again. Anyway, I'm stunned by Dr. Boies's compliment. "Thank you."

"I want to gauge your interest in becoming an examining member of the board."

It was well known that the American Board of Otolaryngology was where the political power was.

"As an examiner," he adds. "To certify the otolaryngologists."

Everybody and his brother wanted to be on the board, the ultimate membership in the old boys' club.

"I'd be honored."

"Good," he says. "That's all." And he goes back to his administrative paperwork.

Over the years, Dr. Boies became less active and his health gradually deteriorated. I encouraged him numerous times to attend to his activities in an office I provided to him. I believed then, as I do now, that the longer you work and keep active, the longer you live, and the more you contribute to this awesome world.

* * * * *

As a board examiner, sometimes I like to tease the young guys. My goal is to get voted "toughest examiner," an honor I'd like to steal from Dr. Joseph Ogura at least once. He wins every year, and I'm tired of it.

I'm in Toronto for the board examinations. I examine the candidate with questions regarding the appropriate diagnosis and patient care. The candidate inspects his patient, and he's doing everything correctly. Occasionally, he glances at me to measure my expression. I keep my eyebrows pinched. Once in a while, I exaggerate a sigh and then scribble madly in my notes. A colony of sweat beads appears on his forehead.

At the end of a perfect examination, the young man nervously asks me how he did. I cannot say. I pause for an unnecessarily long time and flip wildly through my notes. "The results will be sent to you in a few weeks." I say. "Maybe a month." All of my candidates passed.

But for that year at least, I take the title of toughest examiner from Dr. Ogura.

I was elected a board examiner each year from 1968 to 1986. I was asked to re-up for another six years but declined—to give someone else a chance.

In the early days, a board examination was fun, if not exactly standardized or predictable. The questioning was largely left to the whims of the examiner. For the test, the candidate had to examine a live patient, consider the patient's history, and do a physical while we, the examiners, scrutinized. The candidate was given a microscope and slides to formulate a pathological diagnosis, and we pretty much had free rein in terms of asking questions. Most of the candidates were frightened to take the exam, because it's very important to pass so that they can enter the staffs of hospitals, particularly urban hospitals. For a long time, I was in charge of the pathology section and participated in a variety of committees, but I avoided getting mixed up in board politics.

After those early years, complaints ensued indicating that examinations were not objective enough. Although the format of each examination was more fun when the examinations were more loosely proctored, I had to agree that the consensus was accurate. After that, Dr. George F. Reed, department chairman and dean of the SUNY School of Medicine in New York, Dr. Bobby R. Alford of Baylor College of Medicine in Houston, Texas, Dr. James B. (Jim) Snow of the University of Pennsylvania, Dr. Paul H. Ward of UCLA, and I met to standardize the test, in much the same way other serious tests in education and in law are.

After many hours of deliberation and consideration, we developed self-education programs, annual otolaryngologic examinations, monthly quizzes, and branching simulated exercises. Thousands of multiple choice questions were developed by hundreds of members of the academy and then were screened, tested, and entered into a controlled pool to establish hundreds, if not a thousand or more, questions that could be used to standardize the board examination, but that excluded examining a live but very fatigued patient for the ENT test. I'm certain the new format was fair and more objective for the candidates, but it sure was more boring and robotic for the examiners, since we couldn't ad-lib our questions. In the old days, it was rumored that Joe Ogura would sit on a toilet seat in his hotel room sometimes while examining a candidate. I wouldn't do that, but when the Vikings were playing on TV, I would place the candidate in front of the set but have the sound turned off. Anyway, I was grateful for the opportunity and pleased to have been part of creating a more standardized way to examine candidates.

Ultimately, the point of those tough board examinations was to produce a new crop of people who could advance the discipline and further improve people' lives.

* * * * *

In recent years, Dr. Peter Hilger, the son of Jerry Hilger, served as president of the board, while the current chairman and professor at the University of Minnesota, Dr. Bevan Yueh, serves as well. My pride is enhanced.

CHAPTER 22

Clinical Contributions and Selected Honors

Over the years, my team and I at the University of Minnesota have developed many new procedures related to ear diseases.

For years doctors relied solely upon X-rays and CT scans to identify both chronic otitis media and chronic mastoiditis. But I noticed that even the best CT scans demonstrate shadows and sometimes *discrete* shadows that suggest a mass even if there isn't one. These may mean that every patient receives a mastoid operation, even if a cholesteatoma (cyst) isn't found and the operation could be avoided. For this and other reasons, I developed an approach to the operation based on much otopathology research that identified the pathological tissue and anatomical variants, which resulted in a more conservative operation in many cases and didn't require a mastoidectomy. This provides excellent exposure and visualization, so the disease can be treated.

Chronic otitis media in children sometimes led to severe intravenous antibiotics painfully initiated with the patient in the hospital for many days and weeks. We found that a procedure using a flexible surgical approach in such patients could lead to a more conservative operation, for example not requiring hospitalization, or worse, a radical mastoidectomy. This approach has helped many children who otherwise would have had radical surgery, suffering many days in the hospital.

Chronic otitis media in children and adults can lead to an atrophic (collapsed) tympanic membrane and ossicular damage. This can be reconstructed via tympanoplasty for atelectasis, a method I described early on. Since then, many patients have benefited from this technique and had their hearing restored. Exploratory tympanotomy is a procedure that allows an opportunity to see what the problem is and to treat it at the same time, which improves the patient's hearing. Again, understanding the otopathological condition helps us treat the clinical findings.

I also created an operation called the intact-bridge tympanomastoidectomy (IBM) for chronic otitis media and chronic mastoiditis. Formerly, the classic options had been a simple mastoidectomy, a modified radical mastoidectomy, and a radical mastoidectomy. Those three options had been more recently replaced by an intact-wall tympanomastoidectomy, an open-cavity mastoidectomy. We created a combination of those two that results in a smaller mastoid space and a good opportunity for exposure and removal of pathologic tissue. The IBM technique can reduce the problem of a large cavity and usually allows the patient to swim—which, especially in the Land of 10,000 Lakes—is important for a full enjoyment of life. Throughout the development of the IBM, I've had my fellows at my side, learning and participating.

Along with being a board examiner for all those years, I received other gratifying nods to my work in the field of otology. I'll recall a few of the most memorable. The first award I received was in 1960 while I was a resident in Michigan—the Kobrak Award for the research and the paper titled "A High-Frequency Microvibrator: Bioacoustical Effects." Ten years later, in 1970, I was invited to give a lecture at the prestigious University of Tokyo. The department chair there, otolaryngologist Dr. Ichiro Kirikae, was a good friend. He was esteemed as a unique national treasure in Japan. I was a bit nervous, so Dr. Kirikae put me at ease in his conference room, where large bottles of Sapporo beer took the edge off. Subsequently, we've continued to enjoy having a beer together.

In 1973 I was the second American to be guest of honor and honorary member at the Congress of Otorhinolaryngologic Surgery of Japan. Although I'm not tall, only about five feet eight and a half, I felt like a giant when the shorter professors brought me my certificate of honor and flowers on the huge congress hall stage. Outside the hall, Dr. Steven Juhn and I were loitering around, dressed casually, probably both looking like hippies at that time. A man hawking textbooks approached us and wondered if we'd like to buy some. I checked out what he was selling and was surprised to find among his wares a Japanese-language version of the three-volume set of books edited by Dr. Shumrick and me. I didn't buy the books.

Also in 1973 I was invited to Italy, where I lectured at the University of Milan and the University of Padua, the second-oldest university and medical school in Europe. The department chairman was a short, plump, amiable professor named Dr. Michele Arslan. I saw firsthand, as I had earlier in Germany, the power and prestige of the professor and chair in Europe, which contrasted mightily with the way professors were regarded in the States. Professor Arslan had one of the largest ENT programs in Europe, with more than one hundred beds and a staff of forty or more MDs, several of whom were docents in their sixties.

I got to practice my broken Italian while Dr. Arslan and I made rounds with a parade of specialists following. For each patient who had surgery he would call a member of his staff to discuss the "clinical research" on that patient. It was really clinical and not research.

One patient had had major surgery for head and neck cancer the day before, and when Dr. Arslan entered, the patient stood up with intravenous tubes and catheters dangling from him to greet the professor. *"Buongiorno, Professore."*

What respect.

For a time, Dr. Arslan was placing crystals of sodium chloride in the round window niche of the middle ear to treat Ménière's disease while docents were on the floor viewing tapes from continuing ENG tests—why, I don't know. His fingers were long, and a nun had to hold his hand, which had a severe tremor. At night he took me to dinner at a restaurant, and all of the people in the restaurant stood up, bowed, and said *"Buonasera, Professore."* I enjoyed my time in Italy very much and felt a measure of pride that my people were from there.

In 1986 I was the second Brinkman lecturer and honoree at the retirement of Professor W. F. B. Brinkman in Holland. I recall arriving in Nijmegen, a lovely small city, a day early. I decided to walk around to absorb some of the quiet culture. As I wandered, I came upon a music store with loudspeakers blasting Prince, the musician from Minneapolis. The Holland program included the largest live TV course in temporal bone surgery for various diseases. Professors from other countries were invited to perform surgical operations that were televised live. One professor from Germany performed an intact-wall tympanomastoidectomy for extensive cholesteatoma on a young girl. The girl began bleeding briskly during the operation. The German doctor lost his landmarks, lost his way, and had to stop the operation. The doctor was understandably embarrassed, and we were embarrassed for him and not just a little bit sorry for the poor girl.

In 1986 a previous fellow of mine—a Rotary scholar named Luiz Carlos Alves de Sousa who later became head of the ENT department at the University of Ribeirão Preto, a distant suburb of São Paulo, Brazil, and later yet became dean of his medical school—wrote to me. "Dr. Paparella, I intend to name my clinic after you." I objected, but he went ahead and created the Clínica Paparella anyway. All I could say was "Thank you; I'm honored." A couple of years later he and a few other fellows from Brazil created a charitable foundation they also named for me, the Fundação Paparella. The foundation provides free otological care, surgery, and medicine to hundreds of patients per month and fosters research and education at a prestigious national and international level. Wow. I'm very proud of that.

In 1983 Harold Schuknecht, who was still at Harvard, and Jan Wersäll, professor and chairman at Karolinska Institutet in Sweden, and I were guests of honor at the Fifth Asia-Oceanica Meeting in Korea. I recall they took us to a geisha house where, with our shoes off, the geisha girls with white-painted faces fed us, danced for us, and entertained us. No hanky-panky ensued, but I do remember feeling odd and out of my element.

In 1986 my clinic was listed as one of the best in the field of otology in *The Best of Medicine,* edited by H. J. Dietrick and V. H. Biddle, along with the Mayo Clinic in Minnesota.

Dr. Kim Sr. who had been a fellow at the University of Minnesota just before my time then served as professor and chair at the largest prestigious university hospital in South Korea. He made frequent trips to the China Bank in New York City and raised multiple millions to develop a new Seoul National University Hospital. So I was pleased to receive from them a Distinguished Award for Contributions to Research and Medicine in 1989. His son, Dr. Yung Sun Kim Jr., who served as a two-year fellow with me in 1976, later became a professor and chair at the university and a leader of all the major organizations of our field in the world. In 2013 he served as the president of the World Congress of Otolaryngology Head and Neck Surgery, the largest global meeting of practitioners, which happens only every four years. At the next meeting four years later, I was awarded the Gold Medal.

In 1991, along with two other Italian-American physicians from the Twin Cities, Dr. Joseph J. Garamella, a cardiovascular surgeon, and Dr. William Mazzitello, a cardiologist, I received the Italian Heritage Award. We were known as the three Italian musketeers. I also was asked to serve on a Sister City Committee between Saint Paul, Minnesota, and Modena, Italy. One of the best efforts of the committee was to invite Luciano Pavarotti, one of the greatest tenors in the history of opera, born in Modena, to come to the Twin Cities for a wonderful performance.

In 1992 I received an award for dedication to research for otolaryngologic physicians in São Paulo, Brazil, where I performed live TV surgical procedures at the University of São Paulo, the largest university in Brazil. My volunteer nurse was Sady Selaimen da Costa, my former fellow. He became a professor at the university in Porto Alegre and has become a respected leader in Brazil and internationally.

In 1998, I was given the Award of Merit by the best otological society in the world: the American Otological Society. Some of the previous awardees were great contributors to our field, including two former Nobel laureates.

A few more years passed. In that time, I was honored as visiting professor at University of Texas Southwestern in Dallas, but was even more honored to witness the work of Dr. William L. (Bill) Meyerhoff, my former resident and partner, who was professor and chairman there. So many of his graduates were developing successful careers. A similar honor took place when I was invited to Washington University in Saint Louis, where Dr. Richard Chole, another former resident of mine, headed a very strong and successful department. I recall giving a lecture with a big fat lip, the result of an allergic reaction to an ACE inhibitor. It didn't diminish my pride in witnessing firsthand what remarkable contributions Rich was making at that prestigious university.

The aforementioned Dr. David Lim organized a major meeting on recent advances in otitis media. I was a guest of honor in 2001 at the extraordinary meeting in Sendai, Japan. In recent years that poor city and its surrounding areas were tragically devastated by a tsunami and earthquake that occurred off its shoreline. Our friends and colleagues in Japan are strong and capable, and they will survive and thrive.

In 2001 I was guest of honor and lecturer at the 126th Fukuoka and 486th Kyushi Meeting of the Otorhinolaryngological Society of Japan. A large and costly party was held simultaneously for Professor Soda, who was retiring. We were told that each dinner cost at least three hundred dollars per person, and the finest champagne was served, the likes of which I've never seen. To pop the cork of the bottle of specially ordered, expensive French champagne, a gentleman climbed a ladder to the top of the bottle, which was at least nine feet tall.

Also in 2001 I was a guest of honor and the first American otologist invited by the Cuban government to attend the University National Congress of Otolaryngology in Havana. This was when Americans weren't welcomed to Cuba. Old American cars, most badly beat up, were everywhere. We were watched continuously; there was a bug in our hotel bedroom. It was nice for me to see the schoolchildren in uniform; they appeared to attend school in a serious way.

I also was invited each year, over many years, by Iran's minister of health to come and visit. The minister had been a previous fellow of mine and would annually send me the most wonderful pistachios. The people of Iran are great, with a history of making significant contributions to math and science—recall that the Persian Empire dates back six thousand years. They also have a good diet of healthy foods. I've had the privilege of training several Iranians who've become excellent doctors, and I've continued my association with them. I wanted to go, to visit my old student, but I elected not to. I disagree with the Iranian government and its attitude toward our benevolent country.

Prior to and subsequent to the above, I was privileged to speak and be honored at many other universities in the United States and other countries. I've traveled and lectured and been honored many times in Japan and Brazil. Other countries I've had the privilege to visit as part of work include Italy, Austria, Germany, France, Hungary, Holland, Belgium, Russia, China, Korea, Chile, Mexico, Peru, Canada, Egypt, Israel, Switzerland, England, South

Africa, Sweden, Norway, Iceland, Portugal, Spain, Turkey, Argentina, and Finland. For a poor kid from Detroit, I sure get around.

I've been listed in *Who's Who in America and Worldwide* (Marquis); in various lists in *Mpls.St.Paul Magazine* and *Minnesota Monthly*, including "Best Doctors in America," "Best Doctors in America Central Region," and "Best Doctors"; in the Castle Connolly list of top doctors in the United States every year for the past twenty years; and perhaps others.

* * * * *

I have to go back for a moment.

In 1996 Dr. John Shea Jr., who established stapedectomy for otosclerosis, which has restored hearing for millions to date, invited me to celebrate the fortieth anniversary of the stapedectomy operation in Memphis, Tennessee. Dr. Shea had invited about twenty speakers, and I was happy to be the eighteenth, since leaders of the profession were scheduled to speak according to chronological age. The first speaker was Dr. George Shambaugh, who was in his nineties then, and the second was Dr. Howard House, who was also ninety. I was the young kid at eighteenth in line.

My old friend and mentor, Dr. Schuknecht, was there, too. He leaned over my way and said, "Mike, why didn't you stay with me at Harvard? We could have done wonderful things together." He was getting old now, but his eyes were as questioning and curious as ever. He still seemed larger than life to me.

"Harold, have you forgotten? We discussed this already."

"Well?"

"I had to cut the umbilical cord." I stared at him for a moment, feeling a need to capture and remember this moment. Turns out my intuition was on track.

Later that year, in October, Harold died. The man who had been born in Chancellor, South Dakota, had spent two years as a flight surgeon in World War II—earning the Soldier's Medal for saving the life of a pilot caught in a fiery B-24—was gone. The man who had been at the forefront of the renaissance of otological research and practice for decades was gone. The man who had trained so many doctors around the world was gone. Most importantly, my dear friend was gone.

In 1998, I was honored with one of the most poignant, important, and saddest privileges of my life. The International Otopathology Society paid tribute to Harold F. Schuknecht in Boston, and I was humbled to describe his lifetime accomplishments in research, a daunting and impossible task, since he did so much. I did my best, but not good enough in my view. I hope he's relatively pleased, though, wherever he resides.

CHAPTER 23

Developing Partnerships and Relationships

I grew up in a family that never had much money, so I learned to do as much as possible without. But the reality is, no matter how many good ideas you have, no matter how wonderful your work ethic and imagination, money and allies, particularly those with cash to spend, help get those good ideas off the ground. Some people use the wealth they attain to enrich themselves, living in houses that are shrines to their success and driving cars that are flashy advertisements of their bank accounts. Outwardly, I live modestly. Behind the scenes, metaphorically speaking, I pound pavement, searching all the cracks in the sidewalk for money and working deals with individuals and foundations to fund hearing and ear disease research and solutions.

Identifying stakeholders and developing relationships that are mutually beneficial is the key to securing these funds. I've learned how to lead fundraising efforts to improve health by watching, participating, taking small leadership roles, taking some risks, and then taking on larger leadership responsibilities. Like Schuknecht taught me: get in and get wet.

Every single human being is susceptible to a health failure. All of us will have to deal with a major health issue that affects us, or someone close to us, at least once in our lives. Experiencing some kind of hearing loss, for example, is nearly a universal condition. Therefore, it's easy to make that argument to powerful allies by appealing to this reality and inspiring them to help.

In my time at the University of Minnesota, I could sense that a national shift regarding health care was taking place. Toward the end of the late 1980s, a new approach emerged, something that was coined "healthy communities." This shift came out of a deeper understanding that many factors impact a person's overall health and that health solutions need to be more inclusive all around. I began to rethink not only how we trained our physicians, but also how we delivered health care to our patients.

* * * *

Audiology should be an inherent part of the Department of Otolaryngology. Audiometric testing, which assists the diagnosis of hearing loss from diseases of the cochlea (anterior part of the inner ear); electronystagmus testing, which determines the amount of dysfunction of the vestibular labyrinth; and evaluations for hearing aids are all critical components of audiology. Audiological services are absolutely essential to the practice of otology. Unfortunately, an appointment for consultation with audiology used to take a long time, sometimes months, delaying medical diagnosis and management.

Eventually, I suggested that the CEOs of Fairview Hospital, St. Mary's Hospital, and University Hospital and our department contribute twenty thousand dollars to facilitate the development of the Minnesota Regional Hearing Center, a five-thousand-square-foot facility above a commercial store on Franklin Avenue and 25th Avenue South, near Fairview and St. Mary's Hospital. When it was up and running, the center provided service to five thousand patients per year and helped alleviate the delay of audiological services at the university.

Around the same time, while sitting at home alone, I saw a fundraiser by Lions Clubs International on television. It's a wonderful worldwide organization, founded in 1917, that raises money for community services, particularly in the health arena—providing services for people who live with blindness, diabetes, and other health challenges. One of the really great aspects of the Lions Club is that members are forbidden from discussing religion and politics. Fantastic idea. I also appreciate the organizational motto that comes from the name Lions: liberty, intelligence, our nation's safety.

For most of its history, Lions International focused nearly exclusively on providing money and support for research and treatment related to blindness. For years, they were famous for raising money through pancake breakfasts and such to assist research on blindness in universities all over the world. As I watched that televised fundraiser, I decided the Lions should be funding research for hearing disorders and ear diseases. I was going to try to make it happen.

In the late 1970s, I met with Ralph Lyman from Grand Rapids, Michigan, who was then the president of Lions International and thus responsible for the group's charitable activities worldwide. I pestered him until he agreed that Lions International might support research on hearing, not only on blindness. Let this be a lesson to you: People are almost always going to say no the first time. Maybe even the first two or three times. But if your requests are pure and noble, little by little, people or groups that can help will come around to actually doing it. With Lyman's blessing and support, we organized a committee, and a fundraising drive commenced for our Lions International Hearing Center at the Department of Otolaryngology in the University of Minnesota.

A very important ally in this effort was Stan Hubbard, who's listed among the Forbes 400 and is an owner of KSTP, a major TV station in Minnesota plus other media outlets. Hubbard later rocketed into space the first transponders that led the way in satellite TV. Since we had the Lions on board, he was receptive to aiding our fundraising efforts. He provided twenty-four hours of free TV time for three telethons to create the proposed hearing center. The third telethon was abbreviated, personally sponsored with the aid of local manufacturers of hearing aids, since the Lions felt the expense ratio was too large compared to the receipts. The moderator of all those telethons was Shari Lewis with her sock puppet Lamb Chop. Many musical and Hollywood celebrities participated.

The Lions International Hearing Center was the first of its kind in the world, and other Lions Centers have since evolved at many other universities. The Lions continue to provide significant and appreciated support for research and other activities in the Department of Otolaryngology at the U of M.

With the hearing center project, I brought together several networks of support: the hospitals, of course, but also groups from the nonprofit sector, the university system, the private sector, and the media. Finding some success there, I was then tapped for other leadership opportunities.

I served on a Governor's Commission to discuss and recommend the integration and organization of the health sciences, including the University of Minnesota's Medical School, University Hospitals, Public Health, Nursing, Mortuary Science, Dentistry, and Pharmacy, which were all separately identified and independently organized institutions. Elmer Andersen, a respected ex-governor of Minnesota, also served on this committee. Out of this committee's recommendation, the health sciences were organized as a collective chaired by a vice-president of health sciences. Dr. Lyle French, professor and chair of neurosurgery, was the first appointee to the position.

Then I was elected chair of the Council of Clinical Sciences, which referred to the eighteen clinical departments in the medical school. I developed and led a retreat to discuss the authority and structure of the clinical department heads in the medical school and in the university hospitals. The schedule required all eighteen clinical chiefs and chairs to communicate and deliberate in confidential, executive fashion. Each was chair of his or her department in the medical school, as well as chief of his or her clinical department in the hospital.

The vice-president of health sciences, the dean and associate dean, and the hospital administrator were invited to express their ideas to the group of eighteen chairs. Prior to this meeting, we were spoken to by the administrators, and we couldn't leverage our authority as a group regarding policy. Finally, we had the majority of seats at the table and a collective unity. We watched them walk nervously into the meeting room. The traditional barriers and accepted practices and hierarchies were breaking down. And that was a good thing.

CHAPTER 24

Finally, A Real Job, Pa

I call my dad. Faustina answers, says something in Italian and then there's a minute of shuffling and muffled noises, as though she's moving items around, trying to get the phone cord to wherever my dad is. I can picture exactly where he is, in his recliner. But, I'm having trouble picturing *him*. He's getting so old. Finally, I hear him talking to her: "Oh, yes." Once the phone is to his mouth, he coughs and clears his throat.

"Hello, my son."

"Hi, Pa."

He coughs again.

"Pa, you sound terrible. You should go to the doctor."

He scoffs and coughs again. "How is work?" he finally manages to say.

It's no use telling him to see a doctor, so I tell him about my students and my committees and my travels.

"Is this a job?"

"Of course it's a job."

"You go here. You go there. You run around like a chicken with its head cut off."

I chuckle a bit.

"You need a normal job."

"OK, Pa."

* * * * *

Back to my decision to leave the university culture full time and "get a real job." During the early years of my tenure at the University of Minnesota, a small cadre of departmental and other faculty in ophthalmology, otolaryngology, neurology, general surgery, and a few other departments were considered entrepreneurs because they emphasized patient care.

Entrepreneur was a derogatory term. People's eyes would squint and their noses would flutter, as though the very word smelled bad.

I thought differently.

In a university medical school and hospital, research and patient care blend together—one enhances the other. How can you teach patient care if you don't have patients? Patient care leads to questions of research to be studied in laboratories—and through translational research, ideas are brought back to the patient to create innovative, optimized methods of care.

Teaching includes all aspects, and when the balance is right, the university hospital and medical school grow in quality and prestige, all to the benefit of the citizens we serve. On too many occasions, my patients refused to come to University Hospital. They wanted me to care for them in the private sector, where the environment was smaller, warmer, and more intimate. Simple considerations like parking affect where patients want to get their care. I empathized. I wanted patient comfort to be at the center of how we delivered care. This might seem like an obvious notion now, but it's far from the standard policy of earlier years.

In the past, health care modeled a patriarchal system. The doctor and the administrative structure around him knew all and knew best. Subsequently, the patient could often feel infantilized or at the mercy of the doctor's license or power. Little consideration was given to the experience of the patient, getting a clear history, understanding pathology, or even including the patient in decisions about his or her care.

I will admit there's sometimes value to a paternalistic approach. In the 1950s and '60s, major advancements in clinical care and operative solutions to hearing loss and ear diseases were discovered by men (mostly) working in that kind of system. Nobody questioned their authority. The path was cleared for them to solve problems. But I knew there was a way to blend both of those worlds into one that put patients at the center, but also empowered physicians to be scholars, researchers, and practitioners of truly excellent, not just "safe," care.

Schuknecht retired from Harvard in 1987, and a group of individuals suggested I should replace him. At the University of Minnesota, several faculty members suggested I might consider taking on the role of dean of the medical school. But I just didn't want to do either of those things. So having spent many years at several universities, I decided to leave the Big B, the *bureaucracy* of universities, for the Big O, *overhead* and private practice. I decided to try something new, but I intended to keep one foot in the academic sector and the other in the private. I'd be a bridge between those worlds.

On many occasions, my father had naively admonished me. "*Figlio mio, ma ce patza?*" he'd say. "My son, are you crazy? You go to this university, you go to that university, you travel three months a year. When are you going to get a job?" His question resonated. I'd served on the staff of four training programs, three universities, and finally stayed eighteen years on the full-time faculty as professor and chair of the University of Minnesota's program.

I befriended Sister Mary Madonna, CEO of St. Mary's Hospital. Sister Mary Madonna Ashton didn't grow up Catholic, and she wasn't a physician. But she was the most powerful advocate for community health in the state. From the early 1960s to early '80s, she served as the president of St. Mary's Hospital. Then, in 1983, Governor Rudy Perpich tapped her to be Minnesota's first female commissioner of health.

She's a fascinating woman. She was raised in Saint Paul, which has a healthy population of social-justice Catholics, but she was raised Episcopalian. As she tells it, when she decided to convert to Catholicism and become a sister, her mother stopped talking to her. Nevertheless, Sister Mary Madonna felt at peace with her decision, especially since her continued education put her face-to-face with the people who most desperately needed access to health care. Sister Mary Madonna spent her adult life matching the best science in health to its most ubiquitous access for ordinary Minnesotans. Her hands-on approach to working with men with HIV and AIDS during a time when people feared those diseases identified her as a like-minded ally.

As I developed a plan for my clinic, and later a foundation, she encouraged me along the way and agreed to serve on our board. As the site for this new private-practice enterprise, she suggested a parking lot adjacent to St. Mary's Hospital at 701 25th Avenue South in Minneapolis. I produced the down payment, developed a mortgage, and worked with Marlyn Ervasti, the engineer at St. Mary's, and within a few months a small and attractive building named Riverside Park Plaza was added to the hospital grounds.

It had an exterior of white stucco, modeled after a few buildings I had seen in Minneapolis, and many buildings I'd admired in Florida. We made sure the building had an overhang to protect a U-shaped driveway. That way, our patients could get in and out of the clinic without worrying about the rain and snow or whatever else might fall out of the sky in Minnesota. To be extra safe, we added a drive-up in back as well. Above all, I wanted my patients to want to come there. I wanted to make it easy for them to get in the building. We also built a tunnel under the street that connected to the hospital so the staff didn't have to walk outdoors in a Minnesota winter, when there's an almost constant sheet of ice on the sidewalks.

The building was functional and attractive. I liked going there. And I could tell that when my patients entered—when they looked up and saw the wide-open, airy atrium—they felt good there too. This might seem like a small thing, but aesthetics relax patients. The more comfortable they are with the process, from parking their car to easily getting into the building to having a cheerful experience with the front desk, the better their overall patient-care experience.

Also, comparatively, it wasn't even all that expensive to do. While at the U of M, I'd had to raise two to three million dollars to finish the walls and such of a thirty-thousand-square-foot space for clinical and research and administrative space in an existing building. This space became the Lions International Hearing Center. The cost was two hundred dollars per square foot. My new building, from the ground up (including a basement where I built a research lab), cost fifty dollars per square foot. It was as strong as any other university building, with Spancrete separating the five floors. I'll let you come to your own conclusions about the problem of expensive bureaucracy in university settings.

Our clinic, which occupied the second floor of the building, was originally called the Minnesota Ear, Head and Neck Clinic. Later some of my partners overruled me and renamed it the Paparella Ear, Head and Neck Institute. The new building also housed a surgicenter, orthopedics, ob-gyn, psychiatry, and other disciplines.

For years I had dictated all my office charts and kept a separate copy of these clinical records at my own expense, separate from the hospital copy. This allowed the opportunity for me to attract my former patients and have access to all their patient histories. Many chose to make the move with me, so I was off to a running start in private practice.

I retained my relationship with the University of Minnesota. I could have remained at the university full-time for years with a guaranteed salary, but instead I took a risk in private practice. I also maintained a position as professor and chairman emeritus at the university. Teaching is simply part of who I am. Teaching is part of my leadership style. I wanted to continue my principles of supporting research, teaching, and service to burgeoning doctors, albeit with more freedom and a lot less bureaucracy.

At the U of M, I helped train clinical and international research fellows in addition to residents and medical students. In 1985, we created a clinical fellowship program with support from Fairview and St. Mary's Hospitals and have been fortunate to have fellows every year, usually two. These young men and women are fully trained, board-eligible otolaryngologists, often the cream of the crop. They seek additional post-graduate education and experience in office and surgical otology and related disciplines in ENT, which we provide. We also provide research opportunities. All, to my knowledge, have passed the boards. While many have joined university faculties, others have entered private practice. All have been successful in their careers.

Subsequently, universities and the American Board of Otolaryngology Head and Neck Surgery organized

222 • JUST ANOTHER IMMIGRANT'S SON

JUST ANOTHER IMMIGRANT'S SON

a two-year fellowship in which fellows are obligated to spend considerable time in research laboratories, often when their professors do not. If you add up four years of premed, four years of med school, five years of residency, and two years of fellowship training, that amounts to fifteen years of education before you can get a job and attempt to get out of debt. This means the average finishing fellow is thirty-three, the age I was when I became professor and chair at the University of Minnesota, even after I spent two years in the military.

Life is too short, so we elected to continue a one-year fellowship in which I am convinced the finishing fellow has more confidence and experience in otology than some of the two-year programs provide. Moreover, it has been my observation that the residents I trained at the U of M were more confident and adept at ear surgery than are some of the fellows in otology from various other programs around the country.

* * * * *

In 1987, I stick out my neck and arrange a conference, the Otology Surgery Symposium. The biggest names in otology, nationally and internationally, are invited. I don't have an organization, funding, or staff to undertake this level of international meeting. Usually, this type of event is profitable, and the plan is to use any profits to support research at the university. Although invitations had been sent, a few months in advance of the meeting I realize with horror that relatively few participants have signed up to attend the meeting. I scurry around and send more invitations and make more phone calls and finally end up with a good attendance.

When I designed the building, a small auditorium in the lower level was developed for conferences and meetings, with closed-circuit TV connections to the operating rooms for demonstrating live microscopic surgical procedures.

As part of the conference activities, I perform live surgery on a patient with congenital atresia. Congenital atresia is a genetic disorder where the middle ear, mastoid, and external auditory canal do not develop, and usually the auricle (pinna) is malformed—together causing deafness. This is among the most difficult ear operations because surgical landmarks are missing, and dangerous complications, such as facial paralysis due to damage of an aberrant facial nerve or deafness due to anomalies of the middle ear and mastoid, can occur.

While I'm performing and demonstrating the procedure—and it's being shown live on television screens to the conference attendees—Dr. George Shambaugh, a famous otologist, is simultaneously lecturing about congenital atresia to the audience. He's outlining all the dangers of the surgery, and cautioning that most should not attempt it. Though his lecture content causes a lump in my throat, I continue, and the surgery is successful. The patient has a good result with no complications. Thank God.

While I'd hoped to use profits from the conference to support research at the university, instead, I incur a loss. I decide not to host another conference.

Instead I decide to channel the pedagogical energy that inspired the conference in another direction. I would emphasize courses at the National Academy of Otolaryngology Head and Neck Surgery, teach as a visiting professor at universities, and accept invitations to speak at meetings and symposiums.

CHAPTER 25

Treva, Love, and the International Hearing Foundation

My life is centered around my work. And, yet, it feels afloat on the walleye chops. Sometimes, I remember my early years with my dad, mom, brother, and sisters. We probably all romanticize these early years, but I can't help but look back and recall the security and overwhelming sense of love in that house. The love among us was an anchor, so no matter how lean times would get, we didn't feel adrift. I try to be an anchor for my children, and sometimes I wish for a steady fixture at home.

Every month, I pull together a meeting of the board members of the building. On the third floor, there's a dental surgery clinic. The representative of that clinic is a dark and mysterious beauty named Treva. She's bright. She's funny. She's cheery. She's gorgeous. And, she seems made of a metal I'm drawn to like a magnet.

After the meeting ends, I approach her. "How are things going upstairs?"

She looks at me sideways and smiles. "Fine." Her smile widens. "How are things on the second floor?"

"Fine. I did three stapedectomies this morning and then I—" *Shut up,* I tell myself.

She drums her fingers on her coffee mug. "Well, I better go." She saunters out of the room, taking my heart with her.

Over the next weeks and months, I build up my confidence. One day, as I'm coming back from surgery, still dressed in my scrubs, I see her sitting in the atrium reading a book. Her nose is all red, and she looks a little bit miserable.

"Hi, there," I greet her.

She sneezes. "Oh. Excuse me!"

"I'm Dr. Paparella."

"I know that. I'm Treva. We've met several times." I can't be certain, but I'm pretty sure she rolls her eyes at me.

"Right." *I'm an idiot.* "I have a cold too," I offer. "I'm all stuffed up."

"I'm sorry to hear that." She stands. "Well, I better get back to work before the place falls apart without me!"

"Would you like to get coffee sometime?" I blurt.

She turns her beautiful brown eyes on me. The ticking of the clock stops. Waves stop ebbing. Grass stops growing. Bread stops rising. Wind stops blowing. With every fiber of my being, I know the rest of my life depends on the sounds about to emit from Treva's lips. If she doesn't speak soon, I'll pass out from lack of oxygen.

"I guess so," she says.

Somewhere, a volcano erupts. A whale breaches the ocean's surface. A musician strikes a chord. In the galaxy, a star is born. I exhale.

"Why not?" she asks as she darts up the stairs.

I go back to my office. I watch the clock for fifteen minutes. Then I pick up the phone and call her office.

"How about tonight?"

"Tonight?"

"Yes. How about tonight?"

"OK . . ." she says.

"For dinner." There's a long pause, and I'm pretty sure she's going to say no.

"Yes," she says. "You pick."

The only thing that comes to mind is the Italian restaurant in the Holiday Inn near the clinic. I give her the name and address. Hours later, we're giggling like teenagers through two bottles of white zinfandel.

I fall in love with Treva. And she seems to tolerate me pretty well too. In fact, Treva understands the medical world. She understands being a doctor isn't a role I turn off once I get home. She has a hungry mind too, and she's motivated and ambitious. We become inseparable. I hire her away from the other clinic to run the International Hearing Foundation.

We go on as partners for years—for four years to be specific. Our children pester us to make it legal. As do our friends. So, one day, after talking with a patient of mine in the diamond jewelry business, I make arrangements to take Treva back to that old hotel bar and restaurant. She doesn't want to go. She says she's tired.

"You really must meet me there. I have a very important matter to discuss with you."

"Fine," she agrees.

Once there, I order a bottle of white zinfandel. After we're both sufficiently loosened up, I open my briefcase and pull out a magazine full of pictures of rings. I open it to the page I marked, and I push it across the table. "What do you think of this?"

She sips her wine and regards the picture. She blinks several times. I wonder if I should tell her I've already made all the wedding arrangements.

"You've outdone yourself. The answer is yes."

On a warm, beautiful, and sunny day in early October 1992, Treva Crane becomes my wife under the turning leaves and in front of what was supposed to be a small gathering of family and close friends. But our guest list grew, and then grew some more, and when we look out as we say our vows, more than five hundred people are smiling back at us.

Since 1990 Treva, my multitalented wife, has served as director of the International Hearing Foundation (IHF) without compensation. She can do, and does, anything.

The IHF is our baby, and she tends to it as such. Like I do, she believes in the need to raise money to support research at the U of M, particularly the Otopathology Laboratory; train international research fellows and clinical fellows; support projects in other countries; and fund support groups for patients with dizziness or tinnitus; as well as other charitable activities.

The IHF provides education to international research fellows, and service in other countries in Africa and Latin America, where we send doctors. We also provide help in various forms—including free hearing aids to needy patients, free surgery to patients who can't afford it, and so on.

The IHF has a modest budget, but it does a world of good. In association with the Rotary Club, it has provided the best hearing center for deaf children in Chile and a remarkable program in Senegal, where our doctors visit to perform surgery and teach doctors from all over Africa. The professor and chairman at the University of Dakar, and a leader in otology in Senegal, is a previous IHF Fellow, Dr. Malick Diop. Not only does he provide ENT services to patients from Senegal, but to those from surrounding African countries as well. In 2018 a major hearing center dedicated to medical and surgical care for ear and related diseases was established in Senegal with support from the government and the Starkey Foundation, under the direction of Dr. Diop. The center also provides service and education for audiologists and ENT doctors in many African countries.

I can hardly stress enough how important it is to train people from all over the world in the art and science of health care. A doctor from within the culture understands better than an outsider the norms, practices, and environmental factors that might be at play. He or she understands the impediments to the health and wellness of the patient. For instance, a white doctor from America might not understand that patting a child on the head or shaking hands with a Muslim woman might be taboo in that culture, and doing so might discourage people who need care from seeking it.

The IHF and the University of Minnesota have provided opportunities for hundreds of international fellows who come to study at the Otopathology Laboratory at the University of Minnesota. They're also invited to observe clinical, surgical, and academic activities. These fellows have gone back to their countries to offer new skills and knowledge to their many patients—and have taught others who have in turn done the same. They contribute new knowledge to the field by publishing in the medical journals of their countries and international journals. Without attempting to do so, the International Hearing Foundation has spawned sister relationships with other countries, including Chile, Italy, India, and Brazil.

Otolaryngology, and in particular otology and neurotology, represents many diseases occurring in our communities that are grossly underidentified and undersupported. Many people don't realize how devastating those diseases can be to those who suffer with them. Dizziness, hearing loss, deafness, tinnitus—these are common problems that touch most American families in one way or another. The research of the otology renaissance of the twentieth century has been profoundly useful in letting us better understand diagnosis and treatment of ear diseases, but there's so much more to do. Imagine that what we know today about the causes and treatment of ear diseases would fit in the building you're sitting in now, while what we *should* know would cover a space as large as the city surrounding you.

In Minneapolis, we are blessed by corporate giving. Starting with the Dayton-Hudson Corporation (which was absorbed into Macy's Inc.), a number of corporations commit 5 percent of their annual revenue to charity; some contribute 1 percent of their pretax revenues. This has led to helping hospitals and medical needs throughout this community. The Rotary Club has been a very helpful ally of IHF in several of our projects, and we hope our ongoing relationship will continue to spawn new initiatives.

Another important IHF supporter, the Starkey Foundation, is the charitable arm of the largest manufacturer of hearing aids in America. Bill Austin, whose humble life began as the son of a lumber grader and factory worker, demonstrates the great possibility of America. He dropped out of medical school to open a hearing-aid repair shop in his house. Now he's the owner of twenty-one facilities, employing more than four thousand people. He's also a friend, a colleague, a humanitarian, and a philanthropist. He and his wife, Tani, have been instrumental in sustaining IHF's charitable activities in research, education, and service.

* * * * *

I believe, deeply, that giving and helping others is important. When you're a small child, you run downstairs to the Christmas tree because you want a present. But as we grow up, we mature and discover the profound pleasure of giving to others—not just objects, but also time, attention, expertise, and labor.

What's more important? A flashy tombstone—or one good research publication that has the potential to educate and help others for decades? I know what I choose.

Recently, I traveled to Paris, France, to receive a Gold Medal from the ENT World Congress at the Palais des congrès de Paris, not far from the Arc de Triomphe. In many ways, it felt like my career had come full circle. I take pride in having trained or helped train hundreds of specialist MDs in the United States and from other countries. Among them are included residents, clinical fellows and researchers, and international research fellows through the International Hearing Foundation (IHF).

When you raise a child, you have to worry about the birthing process, the terrible twos, the turbulent teen years, and the cost and support of a college education. Then when he or she reaches adulthood, you worry, like my pa did, about your child finding gainful employment and the comfort of a family of his or her own. But as an educator, nurturing is much cheaper, more efficient, and less time-consuming. (Also, you don't have to change diapers.) You can educate fellows or residents in one, two, or five years, and then they're productive in patient care, research, or education. During the decades of their careers, they'll treat patients, conduct research, and teach others—and so the cycle continues. It's like a rock thrown in a still pool with ripples continuing in perpetuity.

I've been privileged to be part of a worldwide family of students, friends, and colleagues. We're like a small universe, ever-expanding ad infinitum through relationships that endure over time and space.

* * * * *

These days, my mornings begin when Treva and I sit down for coffee and breakfast. We talk about our kids, our friends and colleagues, and the IHF. And then I leave for work at the clinic, where I see patients, perform surgery, and try to keep things running smoothly.

Some years ago, in 2008, I was baptized by Father Michael O'Connell at the Basilica of Saint Mary in Minneapolis. My sister Josephine and my friend Giovanna (Mama) D'Agostino served as my godmothers. I'm not fussy about religion, and I see value and similarities in all of them, but it felt right to return to the faith my father left behind in Italy. A few years ago, while I was visiting Italy to accept an award at the International Congress of Ménière's Disease, I was blessed to meet Pope Francis. The day was chilly. I stood in the outdoor mall area of the Vatican with about sixty cardinals, who were quite visually striking in their scarlet robes. Droves of mothers and children had gathered to see and receive a blessing from the pope. He came out and a great cheer erupted from the crowd. He wasn't a very big man, I noted, but he had a huge presence. He walked up and down, shaking hands and exchanging a few words with his followers. Finally, he came to me and took my hand. In Italian, I said slowly, "I pray for you. I pray for the world." He smiled at me and gave me a blessing and assured me that he was praying for me too. It was quite an extended moment.

When I die, I hope they forget my name and only put "Here Lies Dr. Pathogenesis" on my tombstone. I hope to be remembered for a lifetime of focus and devotion to the pathogenesis of various ear diseases. I hope to be known as a significant contributor to an understanding of ear diseases and their management. I hope the temporal bone laboratory continues to be used for research by emerging scholars, so information from collective study can continue to help diagnose and treat the many hundreds of diseases that occur in otology and neurotology. I hope otopathology experiences a reawakening. To that end, one-third of my own estate planning includes basic ongoing support for the otopathology lab.

Epilogue

Melting Pot or Mosaic

The United States is full of immigrants. Here in
Minneapolis in recent years, the largest populations of
Somali and Hmong in the United States have developed.
Each immigrant from every country of the world brought
his/her own cultural DNA, their own foods, music,
habits, and other ethnic characteristics, and they have
been productive in so many ways, to make America the
greatest country in the world today.

   As a result of our multicultural and multiethnic
country, we can enjoy foods from all countries. We can
visit an Italian, Ethiopian, Japanese, or Indian restaurant and sample cuisine from all countries of the world.
We can listen to Italian opera, Cuban or Mexican music,
German or Austrian symphonic orchestrations. We can
appreciate literature and poetry from all countries here
as part of our country, inherent in our culture.

   Immigrants or their children and grandchildren,
or the grandchildren of their grandchildren and so on,
contribute and will contribute to our educational sys-

tem. They serve as teachers in elementary schools or high schools, or as faculty in colleges and universities. In addition to teaching our kids, reading, writing, and arithmetic, they impart an additional color or perspective, which enhances the interest and education of our students. Moreover, the students who attend school with multicultural and multiethnic students benefit not only educationally but also by competing, since first- and second-generation students typically study hard and excel, thus raising the bar for the American student to compete and excel, not to mention the osmotic absorption of other attributes. Ethnic leaders and workers have adopted our entrepreneurial spirit in our US companies, big and small, and as such have contributed to our gross national product, created jobs through innovation in development of products and services, and thus have contributed significantly to our economy.

We live, love, and work in this great "melting pot" of a country, the United States of America. But a "melting pot" connotes a combination of all ethnic ingredients from all countries of the world leading to a uniform, bland, mud-like stew, recognizing that all immigrants and sons and daughters of immigrants first and foremost are and should be proud to be Americans. The popularization of the "melting pot" metaphor is usually traced to a sentimental and very popular play of that name by an immigrant named Israel Zangwill that opened in Washington DC in 1908. But I don't think that phrase completely embodies what is special about America. What is special about American culture isn't its homogeneity but rather its ability to absorb the elements of many cultures.

Furthermore, it's disturbing that the "melting pot" metaphor is a relic of a bygone era when melting different metals together was common in many industries. Melting different metals together produces a desired outcome only if you adhere to a formula. Bronze is copper and tin. Brass is copper and zinc. What results is likely to be flawed and brittle, not strong or useful.

Americans should not surrender our cultural and ethnic identities.

As a friend of mine once told me, wouldn't it be better if we adopted Canada's description of their country? Canada has many immigrants, just as we do in the United States, but they refer to their country as a "mosaic," not as a "melting pot." The mosaic is a unitary, unified and beautiful, holistic and colorful picture of all of the ethnic groups as a proud unit. Although this unitarian depiction of all the immigrants in Canada represents a proud Canadian symbol, each retains an individual secondary ethnic identity. The whole is much better than the individual parts, but the US of A as a "mosaic" instead of a "melting pot" describes the traditional greatness of America while allowing each ethnic contributor its own productive pride and colorful contributions.

My story is about the tiniest piece of the mosaic, or a speck of sand in the national beach of America: "Just Another Immigrant's Son." However, this son, like so many sons and daughters of immigrants, benefited greatly from the opportunity of education and advancement in the United States through hard work, luck, education, skill development, and, ultimately, the chance to give back and help literally thousands and millions of Americans and others. This country of ours is full of immigrants and opportunities.

"In God We Trust" was not only a motto created by our founding fathers, but one experienced and taught by my parents. They had only a few years of education, but understood the miracle of America and the favorable circumstances that exist here. They wanted their kids to discover the American Dream through tenacity and sacrifice. My method of achieving that goal included persistence, optimism, and never giving up.

While my chosen career was otolaryngoly, and specifically otology, certainly similar opportunities and methods of achieving success exist for every career in this country. I hope in some small way that my story will encourage other immigrants' sons and daughters to fully embrace this great land of opportunity.

Acknowledgments

La Famiglia, First and Foremost

I was blessed to be born into a poor ghetto and into a great family. Further, I was blessed with the privilege of many fine relatives, all products of relatively recent immigrations. Not a single one has been a detriment to society, and all in their own individual ways have made significant contributions to this great mosaic of America. They're kind and generous people.

My father was capable and self-educated. He could do so many things—start his own dry-goods and grocery store, tear down a car, install a furnace and its connections, and he served as a lay preacher in the Italian Gospel Hall. He and my mother insisted on education for their four kids, and they sacrificed to make that happen. They would quarrel with each other sometimes, and they didn't spare the rod. (It was actually a big wooden spoon in the kitchen called the "board of education," although my father would use his belt from time to time.) They loved us and supported us, and we all helped each other. Each of us married and had children and most of the children married and had children, and the beat goes on.

Pa passed away in 1981, of complications from respiratory illness. I can still hear his voice in my ear, giving me advice about this and that. Mostly I hear him saying, "Son, you will be a doctor." And, of course, his ongoing refrain, "Go get a real job." Faustina moved to Italy to be near her family. Steve, my son, and I traveled there and got to say hello to her.

My oldest son, Mark, married Ann, a lovely and smart young lady. Mark and Ann both attended Macalester College. Ann is a special education paraprofessional, and Mark has developed proficiencies in the complicated world of business in the medical arena. He heads the business office in our clinic and has consistently done a good job. Mark and Ann have two children: Laura, a summa cum laude graduate of the University of St. Thomas who also earned a master's degree in social studies, and Benjamin, a graphic artist.

My younger son, Steven, a bit later in life, married Misty, who studied sociology and criminal justice at the University of Colorado. Though they are now divorced, they happily co-parent a daughter, Miliah, and a son, Mauro, named after me. Incidentally, that wasn't my idea—but, boy, am I proud. They're both excelling in school and sports. Steven went to Arizona State and then acquired a business degree with good grades at a college in Michigan. He has participated in various entrepreneurial industries, once running his own carpet-cleaning business and a series of seafood restaurants called Joey's Only Seafood. Currently he's working as a manager of a Bed, Bath & Beyond.

Both Steven and Mark have always done a good job at their chosen endeavors. Sometimes I think they were smart to not want to spend fifteen or more years to become a professional MD, for example.

As mentioned, Rebecca Hendrickson became my second wife. She was brought up on a Finnish farm, and as a young girl traveled Europe extensively with other college kids with backpacks. Together, in 1982, we adopted three-month-old Lisa from Chile. Lisa, who's smart and articulate, earned very good grades in school, and went on to acquire a BA and an MA, and now serves as a family counselor. Curiously, when she was in high school she went out for the boys' varsity football team and, shocking as it may seem, she made the team—partly, I think, because she's strong-willed and convinced the coach. She played on the line, of all things, and her team won the state championship. Lisa married her husband, Mark, and they have two lovely young twin girls, Lucy and Lily. They have bright eyes that seem so intelligent, absorbing the world around them.

On my next matrimonial go-around, things worked out really well. I met and married Treva Crane. Treva's marital history was similar to mine. Her first husband developed cerebral disease, perhaps an aneurysm, and he died too early, similar to Lynne. They had two children, Shelley and Brad. Shelley married Mark Raiola and they had two smart and lovely daughters, Alyssa and

Jenna. Shelley works as an administrative and health assistant at an elementary school, and Mark was a security computer professional for Ecolab and other companies. Sadly, Mark died much too early. Brad, who loved to ski, went to Vail, Colorado, after leaving the nest, and he's still there. He won an award for being the best mountain groomer in Colorado.

Treva, a beautiful person inside and outside, is my love, wife, and life. When she was younger, she participated in and ran beauty pagaents. She has multiple talents and has done and can do many things. For example, prior to our marriage, she ran a resort in Wisconsin and at the same time managed a dental office, raised five young children (two of her own), and served on the Chamber of Commerce, which organized and ran special community events—for example, Treva helped them bring country-western stars, such as Kenny Rogers, The Judds, and the Oakridge Boys, to perform at local venues. She's also a good cook. She used to cook all sorts of wild game her previous husband would bring home. As an example, she'd cook bear meat and organize a feast.

With all these and other attributes—besides being beautiful and giving—no wonder she was more than qualified to be part of my active "do this, do that," "go here, go there" life. I've often referred to her as my Tim Allen, because she can fix things around the house and does so on a regular basis, much better than I can. I always ask if I can help, and she always declines. So I keep asking. She also loves to work in the garden, growing tomatoes and herbs. Our family, especially me, loves her, and she has been giving to all. And, of course, Treva also directs the International Hearing Foundation, a position for which she receives no compensation and one liability: she lives with me and gets to sleep with the boss!

* * * * *

While I believe family is first and foremost, have I been an ideal father and husband? Probably not. Although I meant to be, when tragic or difficult times happen, my response is to work harder to support my family and my principles, while at the same time doing my best to take care of the family. I am not unique in this regard, as many have done the same thing. While there is a sense of accomplishment, nevertheless there is also a sense of guilt. The greatest sense of remorse relates to Lynne's disease and the fact that I truly wanted her to stay in Minnesota, to take care of her and help her, but her family insisted they could do better in Detroit. But it was a difficult situation for my sons.

Mark and Steve went through very difficult times with long-term scars, but I felt helpless because if I called or visited Michigan, it made matters worse and would result in a negative reaction from Lynne. My sincere apologies to them are heartfelt. As years passed and as I and my children mellow, relationships improve. But I could have done better.

Freud once said, "Life equals work plus love." Love equals mostly family. On the work side, I probably deserve an A-. On the love and family side, I hope my kids would have given me a C- in the past, and would agree I later maybe worked myself up to a B.

I have traveled widely throughout the world, and the more I travel, the more I come back and realize that the Twin Cities, and Minneapolis in particular where I live, have remarkable opportunities for culture, for recreation, for beauty and enjoyment. We have hundreds of lakes in the Twin Cities area, including twenty-two in Minneapolis per se. In fact, our home is really close to a lovely lake called Lake of the Isles. We live close to downtown and have the opportunity to see a world-class orchestra, the Minnesota Orchestra, under the current conductor Vanska, or to go to the Guthrie Theater to see plays of equal caliber that one could see on Broadway, and many other opportunities for theater, culture, courses, reading, music, recreation, exercise. For example Minneapolis has been named the #1 bicycle city in the United States. I was a little surprised when I learned that the "little apple," Minneapolis, has the second most theater seats per capita, behind the "big apple," New York City.

The economy has always been better than other cities', particularly in the Midwest, since we have a diversified economy and currently have many Fortune 500 companies in this area that provide opportunities for work, life, and enjoyment. Most of the corporations in this community provide a significant percentage of their pretax profits to support the arts and other important charitable endeavors, which helps explain the rich diversity of culture and other wonderful living opportunities that exist in this area. I have often said that if I had more time, I would have enjoyed working for the Chamber of Commerce, to help promote this area, which is certainly a lovely one to live and work in. Perhaps one day I will.

I have found that boredom is not a problem here. With so many activities and experiences available, it is impossible to keep track of them, let alone participate in so many opportunities. People, especially in places like Florida, love to talk about our cold winters, but temperatures in Embarrass, Minnesota, hundreds of miles north, are far different from those in Minneapolis. More romance and productivity occur during winter days and evenings in Minnesota than in southern climes of the United States. Moreover, we can experience sometimes two or three seasonal climates, sometimes within a two-day period. Certainly not boring. I do feel blessed.

My gratitude for my opportunities and my family is tremendous. There are so many people to thank I don't know where to start. How do I begin so it can be done appropriately? One of the first things I would say is a thank-you to my country and the Constitution that has provided us the best country for opportunity to grow and to develop, to have a good life, to have prosperity not only to live comfortably but so that we can help others.

My parents came from Italy expecting that the streets were paved with gold. They were not paved with gold; they were kind of dirty, with bumps and holes, but this country provided them with opportunity. My dad worked in a coal mine originally, and then he worked at other jobs until he was drafted into the US Army, and almost died fighting for America. The main thing our parents and this country gave my siblings and me was the opportunity to have an education. With that opportunity we were able to build our families, our jobs, our careers, our objectives, which allowed us to help first ourselves and our families, but then others.

I would certainly therefore thank not only my country, but I would thank my parents, my mother and father who suffered their children and who insisted that their boys get a college education, which was unique in our whole neighborhood growing up in Detroit, since we were the only two, my brother and I, who did so. Education was stressed, and that led us to learn more about the world and to have the opportunity to get good jobs.

I would also thank my role models, particularly Dr. Harold Schuknecht. There were others, but I would again put him at the top of the list, since he was so dedicated to patient care, research, and education that it was a contagion that affected me, and I then did my best to follow in his footsteps. This led to a world of opportunity for me in research, education, and service. I want to thank my other teachers during my residency, Dr. Dill and Dr. Bolstad, and I include Dr. Maxwell, the head of the Department of Otolaryngology at the University of Michigan, who at least scared me enough so that I went to another institution for training. I would also, as we have done in presenting the Paparella Award at the national academy, thank our many teachers such as Bill House, John Shea, Howard House, and others.

Dr. Theodore Walsh was a chairman at Washington University in Saint Louis for many years, and he was followed by Dr. Joe Agura, a well-known head and neck surgeon. Dr. Walsh was a well-regarded otologist. I have to thank them because, unbeknownst to me, they were the ones who proposed me for all the major societies, including the Otological Society and the Collegium, and I didn't know them well but they were kind enough to propose me for membership in those important groups. I would also thank all the people who have helped me work in the clinic. There are so many I can't thank them all, but I will single out Joann Epley, who was my nurse in the clinic, and Patty Burggraff, both of whom came with me from the university.

I would thank my university associates at Henry Ford Hospital, Harvard, Ohio State, the University of Minnesota. It was a big moment in my life when the chairman of neurology and the search committee appointed me to be the chairman of otolaryngology at the University of Minnesota. That was a major turning point that allowed me to accomplish many of the objectives I mentioned earlier. I thank those who developed the Twin Cities with their many opportunities for education, culture, recreation, parks, rivers, and so forth as a desirable place to live and to grow in. The more I travel around the world, the more I appreciate Minneapolis as a wonderful city I am privileged to live in.

I thank once again Bill Austin for helping us with our IHF research programs, and thank Stan Hubbard, who helped us with the telethons that raised money for the university. I would thank my many past residents and clinical and research fellows for teaching me as much if not more than what I might have shared with them. I also sincerely thank the staff and faculty at the Paparella Ear, Head, & Neck Institute and the Department of Otolaryngology at the University of Minnesota, with special thanks to the supportive board of the International Hearing Foundation (IHF).

To turn to this book, I'm grateful to Nicole Helget, a successful author of various publications. She transposed some of my rote medical writings by interjecting a storytelling aspect for the readers' interest. She also provided interesting historical background information to some of my life events. My sincere thanks also are extended to Dr. Norman Berlinger, a friend and colleague who has published medical articles nationally including in the *New York Times*. In addition, I thank Marcia Neely, a friend and a great writer (her novel, *Deep Grass Roots*, recently won the Benjamin Franklin Award for historical fiction) for her forbearance in reviewing this manuscript. Most importantly, my gratitude and appreciation is extended to Beaver's Pond Press in general and Alicia Ester in particular for guiding me through my first experience in publishing a book designed not only for the medical profession, but also for the public and patients, who this book is for and who it is all about.

I close by thanking my children for bearing with me all these years under difficult circumstances and Treva, a wonderful, supportive, loving wife, who has made my life more enhanced and beautiful so I could do my work and try to help others. In summary, I thank all those who have given me the opportunity to work, but I equally thank all of those who have given me the opportunity to love.

Now, back to work.

The Importance of Otopathology Research

Would you like to learn more about it? Would you like to help?

As mentioned often throughout these pages, translational research and especially otopathology research, have been extremely important as the best way to help thousands, indeed millions of patients with common and serious ear diseases that can cause deafness, infection, vertigo, and other debilitating symptoms. While there should be at least hundreds of such research facilities, only three exist in the world. This critical research from our otopathology laboratory at the University of Minnesota helps ear specialists understand better ways to diagnose and treat their patients and helps lead to the discovery of new diseases. All proceeds from the sale of this book will support otopathology research at the University of Minnesota.

If you have a serious ear disease, I encourage you to donate your temporal bones for research. The donation doesn't result in disfigurement when a complete autopsy is done. The study of temporal bones is a vital way to significantly support critical otological research, which contributes to knowledge that has the potential to help patients with devastating ear diseases. To get more information, please contact the Otopathology Laboratory at the University of Minnesota:

Otopathology Laboratory
Department of Otolaryngology, University of Minnesota
Lions Research Building, Room 210
2201 6th Street South East
Minneapolis, MN 55455
www.pehni.com/practice/otopath_lab.htm
612-624-5466

Your financial support is another critical way you can help sustain ongoing research into the common and rare diseases that affect millions of people worldwide. Donations and support of the Otopathology Laboratory can be sent to the University of Minnesota Foundation – Fund #15426. The address is:

University of Minnesota Foundation – Fund 15426
200 Oak Street South East, Suite 500
Minneapolis, MN 55455

About the Author

Michael Mauro Paparella, MD, is the professor, chairman emeritus, and director of the Otopatholgy Laboratory at the University of Minnesota and president of the Paparella Ear, Head, and Neck Institute. He is also the founder of the International Hearing Foundation. He has published more than 720 articles and 65 books. His dedication to clinical ear research has greatly benefited patient care for many individuals, including those who have incapacitating Ménière's disease or severe chronic ear infections. His great satisfaction is having trained hundreds of ear specialists throughout the world who have become leaders in our profession and who continue to be productive in education, research, and patient care.